WHO'S BETTER, WHO'S BEST IN COACHING?

Setting the Record Straight on
the Top 50 NFL Coaches in History

STEVE SILVERMAN

SPORTS
PUBLISHING

Sports Publishing books may be purchased in bulk at special discounts for sales promotion, corporate gifts, fund-raising, or educational purposes. Special editions can also be created to specifications. For details, contact the Special Sales Department, Sports Publishing, 307 West 36th Street, 11th Floor, New York, NY 10018 or sportspubbooks@skyhorsepublishing.com.

Sports Publishing® is a registered trademark of Skyhorse Publishing, Inc.®, a Delaware corporation.

Visit our website at www.sportspubbooks.com.

10 9 8 7 6 5 4 3 2 1

Library of Congress Cataloging-in-Publication Data is available on file.

Cover photo credit AP Images

ISBN: 978-1-61321-764-1
Ebook ISBN: 978-1-61321-787-0
Printed in the United States of America

CONTENTS

VINCE LOMBARDI

There is little doubt that Vince Lombardi was the most compelling coach in the history of the NFL, and perhaps the greatest coach and leader in the history of all North American sports, let alone professional football.

His talent and prowess were not in his ability to draw up explosive and scintillating plays. There were many coaches who had far more to offer in that area, but when it came to getting his players to prepare well and execute at their best on an every-week basis, Lombardi set a standard that no other coach has been able to sustain.

Lombardi also had an eye for execution. When his teams practiced, he made sure that each player got it right before he moved on to the next play.

That was the Lombardi way, and those who played for him in Green Bay from 1959 through 1967, or in Washington in 1969, quickly learned that there was only one way to get things done. Those who chose to try to get by or to put one over on Lombardi did not last long under his watchful eye.

Lombardi had been the offensive coordinator of the New York Giants under Jim Lee Howell in the late 1950s. While Lombardi coached the offense, Tom Landry ran the defense and the two competed hard against each other, something that would play out quite a bit during the 1960s.

There was a strong impression that Lombardi would eventually become head coach of the Giants, and that would have pleased the New Jersey native quite a bit. However, the lowly Green Bay Packers came calling in 1959, and Lombardi seized the opportunity even though the Packers had not had a winning season since 1947.

It was assumed that Lombardi was inheriting a mess of a team, but he didn't see it that way once he arrived at training camp that year. Instead, he saw the Packers as a fairly talented team that had lacked direction and discipline.

Lombardi provided both of those characteristics and did it with gusto. He simplified the Green Bay offense and had his team work on the basic fundamentals of the game—blocking and tackling. The power sweep was his bread and butter play, and he would run it again and again in practice so that each player knew where he was supposed to be as a matter of instinct.

That play featured the offensive guards pulling out from the line of scrimmage and running toward the sidelines, where they would kick out opposing linebackers or defensive backs and seal off an alley for the running back to attack with gusto.

Lombardi said the power sweep was his top play because each of his eleven players was required to do his job in order to make it work. The actions of the team, rather than the players as individuals, is why Lombardi loved the game.

"It's all about teamwork," Lombardi said. "Individual commitment to a group effort—that is what makes a team work, a company work, a society work, a civilization work.

Lombardi's influence on the Packers was felt immediately. He drove his men hard in his initial training camp at St. Norbert's College in DePere, Wisconsin, but his players also knew there was something different about this coach. Angry, gruff, demanding, and intimidating, Lombardi also cared deeply about his players. It may not have shown on the surface, but his players learned this quickly.

Green Bay went 7-5-0 in 1959, and the rest of the league took notice of what Lombardi was doing with his team. He turned Bart Starr, a 17th-round draft choice selected in 1956, into his starting quarterback. Starr may not have been a strong-armed quarterback, but he was an accurate passer who played the game with intelligence. He also had substantial leadership ability, which Lombardi recognized and appreciated.

In addition, he had two gifted running backs in Paul Hornung and Jim Taylor, and both of them knew how to run the power sweep. The defense was tough, mean, and aggressive. By the 1960 season, the Packers were on their way to becoming a juggernaut. They won the West Division with an 8-4-0 record, setting the stage for their matchup with the Philadelphia Eagles in the NFL Championship game.

Green Bay dropped a 17-13 decision, but the Packers had the ball in the final moments and came up just short in their bid to win the game.

The Packers never lost another postseason game under Lombardi.

Green Bay became a dominant team in 1961 and '62, as they would go 11-3 and 13-1 in the next two seasons. They would overwhelm the Giants 37-0 in the '61 championship game and repeat their title the following year with a closer 16-7 win over the Giants.

Lombardi strived to win championships, but he was never satisfied because winning a particular game or a title was never his long-term goal. He was all about achieving perfection, and while that can never be sustained on the football field, his demanding practices meant that there would never be any satisfaction among his players or his coaches.

He made them all work to a higher standard, and it paid off dramatically.

While the Packers did not win the title in '63 or '64, those failures just prepared his team for what was to come. Green Bay finished 10-3-1 in 1965, and that left them tied with the Baltimore Colts for the West Division title.

That meant the two teams had to engage in a playoff to break the tie, and neither team had its starting quarterback. The Colts, coached by young Don Shula, had neither starter Johnny Unitas nor backup Gary Cuozzo, while Starr was injured for the Packers. Green Bay backup quarterback Zeke Bratkowski led the Packers to a 13-10 overtime victory.

The Packers pounced on their opportunity and rolled over the Cleveland Browns 23-12 in the NFL Championship game.

The following year, the Packers were a sensational team and won the West Division with a 12-2 record. Lombardi took his Packers to Dallas to play Landry's Cowboys in the NFL Championship game, and the two teams slugged it out for 60 minutes.

The Packers had played one of their best offensive games and had a 34–27 lead in the late going at the Cotton Bowl, but the Cowboys had the ball and Don Meredith was driving them to possibly tie the score and send the game to overtime.

However, linebacker Dave Robinson stormed into the backfield on a 4th-and-goal play from the two-yard line, and Packers defensive back Tom Brown was able to intercept Meredith's wobbly pass.

That clinched the title for the Packers, and it gave them a chance to play in the first Super Bowl against the Kansas City Chiefs.

There was intense pressure under Lombardi. He was not only trying to get the Packers an important win, but he was also coaching to uphold the honor of the NFL over the upstart American Football League. While the Packers were considered the better team, it was basically a no-win situation for Lombardi. If he and the Packers won, they would have been doing the expected. If they lost, they would have let down the entire NFL.

The Chiefs played the Packers tight for a half and trailed just 14-10 after 30 minutes, but the Packers took charge in the second half and pulled away for a 35–10 victory. After the game, Lombardi was visibly relieved, and he took a swipe at the Chiefs and the AFL, saying there were five or six NFL teams that were better.

The following year, the Packers met the Cowboys in the NFL title game again. But this time, the game was played in painful 16-below conditions at Lambeau Field in Green Bay. The brutal weather made this sensational game even more of a classic, as the Packers were pushed to the limit by the Cowboys and won the game on the final play when Starr scored on a quarterback sneak over guard Jerry Kramer.

It was a play that would symbolize Lombardi's coaching during his run in Green Bay—simple, yet effective and decisive when the Packers needed it most.

A second-straight trip to what would soon be known as the Super Bowl resulted in another relatively easy Green Bay victory. The Packers overpowered the Oakland Raiders 33-14.

However, the news came after the game that Lombardi decided to step away from coaching. While it was surprising, it did not send shock waves throughout the NFL. Lombardi's success in the coaching profession allowed him to step away knowing he had brought the Packers to the top of the football world—and kept them there.

He felt he had met his challenges, and therefore it was time to figure out what he wanted to do next with his life.

However, after a year away from coaching, he decided he wanted back at it and took a job as coach of the Washington Redskins.

The Redskins were coming off back-to-back losing seasons, and few thought Lombardi could do much with the talent he had to work with. However, the Redskins turned things around with a 7-5-2 record, and enthusiasm was at a high level as the team moved into the offseason.

But Lombardi did not coach the team in 1970, as he was diagnosed with cancer and died shortly thereafter.

Lombardi did not have the chance to finish the job he started with the Redskins, but players like Sonny Jurgensen, Charley Taylor, Sam Huff, and Pat Fischer believed he could have taken them to the championship if he had stayed healthy.

Lombardi's legacy has since been cemented by the NFL, as he gained entry into the Hall of Fame posthumously in 1971, and the league named its iconic championship trophy after him.

He was a tough, demanding, and accomplished coach who brought out the best in anyone around him. His legend lives on in the lives he touched, and he set a standard for excellence that no NFL coach has ever matched.

For the record

Vince Lombardi
Hall of Fame, 1971
Regular-season record: 96-34-6, .738
Postseason record: 9-1, .900
Two Super Bowl victories
Three NFL championships

#2

BILL BELICHICK

There is no limit to the amount of work Bill Belichick will do when it comes to winning.

He is a grinder who will study film of his opponents, will work with his own team closely, and will come up with innovative game plans that are nearly impossible for opponents to predict ahead of time.

What Belichick won't do is explain to the media and fans what he is doing, because he is not going to give anything away to his competition. If he wanted to build a friendly and informative relationship with the media, that would take away from the competitive advantage that he has built during his twenty years as an NFL head coach.

During those twenty years—fifteen with the New England Patriots through the 2014 season and five with the Cleveland Browns—he has won four Super Bowl titles. He has earned his status among the greatest minds who have ever coached in the NFL, and he refuses to be satisfied.

Belichick is all about winning, and that is his addiction.

That's what separates Belichick from many of the other elite coaches in NFL history. Once he wins, he is not trying to maintain his team's status. He looks at each season as a separate entity, working tirelessly to get to the top and then starting again the next season.

"If you are a player who can help the Patriots win, you have a chance to make this roster," Belichick said. "It doesn't matter how much money you make or where you were drafted. It doesn't matter what you did last year. If you can help us win now, you belong here. If you can't, you won't be on this team."

Belichick was not a stellar head coach by most standards during his first five years with the Cleveland Browns. However, Cleveland made the playoffs with an 11-5 record in 1994—his fourth season with the Browns—and beat the Patriots in their first playoff game before being eliminated by the Steelers.

A tough 5-11 season followed in 1995, and Belichick was sent packing. However, when he took his second head-coaching job with the Patriots in 2000, he was ready to lead his team to the top of the football world.

Belichick was one of the finest defensive minds in football before he was given either of his head coaching opportunities. His ability to figure out the game plan often gave his teams a better opportunity to win.

Belichick started off as an assistant with the Baltimore Colts in 1975 and worked his way up the football ladder. While he had many positions along the way, with the Detroit Lions, Denver Broncos, and New York Giants, he came into his own as defensive coordinator with the Giants.

Belichick served in that position from 1985 through 1990, and while he had perhaps the game's best linebacker in Lawrence Taylor on his side, he devised a defense that allowed the Giants to dominate. New York won Super Bowls following the 1986 and 1990 seasons, and New York's victory over Buffalo in '90 was a great feather in Belichick's cap.

The Bills were the most explosive team in football that year, and had earned their spot in the Super Bowl after defeating the Oakland Raiders 51-3 in the AFC title game. The Giants were playing with backup quarterback Jeff Hostetler in the lineup, and Belichick had to find a way to keep the Bills from making big plays and lighting up the scoreboard.

Not only did he do that, but he impressed on head coach Bill Parcells the Giants' need to hold on to the ball and keep the ball out of the Bills' hands. Even though the Giants appeared to be overmatched, the game plan worked perfectly as New York escaped with a 20-19 victory.

By the time Belichick was hired by the Patriots in 2000—after a strange dance with the New York Jets that saw him accept their head coaching position and reject it 24 hours later—Belichick had earned his "doctorate" in professional football.

The same year that Belichick came aboard in New England, the Patriots drafted Tom Brady out of the University of Michigan in the sixth round. Brady was hardly a sure thing to earn a spot on the New England roster, but he quickly impressed the Patriots coaching staff with his skill and preparation.

While he basically sat and watched in 2000 when the Patriots went 5-11, he was fully prepared to play in the 2001 season. New England had a solid starter in Drew Bledsoe, but Brady prepared every week as if he would get the call.

When Bledsoe went down with a severe injury that season, Brady took over and performed far above expectations. The Patriots won the AFC East title with an 11-5 record, and Belichick was facing a tough decision.

Once Bledsoe recovered, he had to decide whether to give the veteran quarterback his starting position back, or to let Brady remain under center. Convention indicated that Bledsoe shouldn't lose his job because of an injury, but Belichick has never been a coach to go by convention.

He trusted his gut, and stuck with Brady. The Patriots continued to roll in the postseason, as they won playoff games over the Oakland Raiders and Pittsburgh Steelers (Bledsoe relieved Brady in that game) and went to the Super Bowl.

The upstarts from New England were expected to be cannon fodder for the heavily favored St. Louis Rams, but Belichick's defense got physical and limited receivers like Isaac Bruce and Torry Holt and also found a way to keep Kurt Warner and Marshall Faulk in check.

Most importantly, Brady was able to lead the Patriots' offense successfully, throwing for 145 yards and a touchdown while keeping it clean on the interception side of the ledger. He also led the Patriots to a game-winning field goal in the final seconds.

Belichick's Patriots were not through at that point, as they would win two of the next three Super Bowls, with close victories over the Carolina Panthers and Philadelphia Eagles.

All three of their Super Bowl victories were tight ones, so the Patriots did not get put in the same category with previous NFL dynasties like the Pittsburgh Steelers, San Francisco 49ers, and Dallas Cowboys.

Nevertheless, Belichick's team would win as those teams never did. The Patriots reeled off 14 consecutive winning seasons beginning with their 2001 championship year, and they have been to the postseason in all but two of those seasons (2002 and 2008).

However, they could not win another Super Bowl title until 2014, when they rallied with fourteen fourth-quarter points to beat the Seattle Seahawks in Super Bowl XLIX.

Prior to that, they lost two Super Bowls to the New York Giants following the 2007 and 2011 seasons. The loss in 2007 was particularly noteworthy, because the Patriots were 16-0-0 in the regular season and had swept their playoff games before New York used a spectacular pitch and catch from quarterback Eli Manning to unheralded wide receiver David Tyree to key the upset.

While Belichick's consistent excellence has allowed him to become one of the sport's coaching greats, his career has been steeped in controversy.

Belichick has often been accused of pushing the rules to the limit. Both he and his team were fined and the Patriots lost draft picks after the NFL determined that New England illegally filmed opponents' practice sessions to give the team a strategic edge.

After the 2014 AFC Championship victory over the Colts, the "Deflategate" controversy blew up, as eleven of the twelve footballs used by the Patriots were reportedly not inflated to the proper standards.

At the time that this book went to press, no determination of guilt had been assessed by the NFL, but many observers believed that Brady, Belichick, or some other New England employee played a key role in deflating the footballs. Brady and Belichick denied any wrongdoing.

Belichick may not like to share his ways with the public or elaborate when he speaks to the media. However, when it comes to winning football games and championships and preparing for any and all possibilities, he walks shoulder to shoulder with Lombardi.

For the record

> **Bill Belichick**
> Regular-season record: 211-109-0, .659
> Postseason record: 22-9, .710
> Four Super Bowl victories

#3

TOM LANDRY

The man in the fedora and the impeccable suit stood on the Dallas Cowboys sidelines for the first twenty-nine years of the franchise's existence. Under his leadership, the Cowboys went from a laughingstock of an expansion team to America's Team.

The only professional sports rival the team has had in terms of popularity throughout the decades is the New York Yankees, and the Bronx Bombers had a long head start in which they had icons like Babe Ruth, Lou Gehrig, Joe DiMaggio, and Mickey Mantle represent them.

Landry shepherded the Cowboys every step of the way, and it was clear he was destined for greatness when he was named head coach of the expansion team prior to the 1960 season. Landry had been a defensive back with the New York Giants, and while he was still in uniform when playing for head coach Steve Owen, he was asked to implement the Giants "Umbrella" defense and became a coach on the field.

When Jim Lee Howell took over for the embattled Owen, Landry officially became a player coach and then a full-fledged defensive coordinator. While Landry was running the defense for the Giants, Vince Lombardi ran the offense. The association of Landry and Lombardi working together undoubtedly gave the Giants the best set of assistants any team has ever had.

Landry was more than ready to compete with the best minds in the game, but it took a while for the expansion Cowboys to get competitive. Owner Clint Murchison had Tex Schramm as his general manager and Gil Brandt as his head of personnel, along with Landry as his head coach, and those three turned the Cowboys into a formidable franchise.

The Cowboys suffered through five consecutive losing seasons through 1964, but they finished at .500 with a 7-7 record in 1965. After undergoing a 2-5 first half, the Cowboys reversed that record in the second half of the season and showed they were ready to become one of the NFL's elite teams.

They lived up to that promise the following year when they went 10-3-1 and finished first in the NFL's East Division. That success set them up for the championship game against Lombardi's Packers in the last year of the NFL's two-division setup.

The Packers were the league's dominant team at the time, and they came into the Cotton Bowl expecting to take care of the Cowboys with few problems. However, Landry's Cowboys were becoming an offensive juggernaut with Don Meredith at quarterback, Don Perkins and Dan Reeves at running back, and explosive Bob Hayes at wide receiver.

Landry had Lombardi in a cold sweat as the Cowboys had the ball on the doorstep of a tying touchdown in the final moments of regulation time. Meredith, harassed by Willie Davis and the Packers' defensive front, hurled the ball into the end zone, where it was intercepted by Tom Brown to preserve Green Bay's 34–27 victory.

The following year, the two teams met in perhaps the most famous NFL Championship game of all time in Green Bay. The temperatures dropped to a ferocious minus–16 degrees, and Landry's Cowboys had a 17–14 lead until the game's final play. That's when Green Bay guard Jerry Kramer bowled over Dallas defensive tackle Jethro Pugh, and quarterback Bart Starr followed the block into the end zone with the game-winning touchdown in a 21–17 triumph.

The Cowboys gained many new fans in that heroic defeat. They had played Lombardi's Packers nearly even in two championship games, and many thought the Packers were the greatest NFL team of all time.

Landry and the Cowboys would win consistently from that point forward. The Cowboys earned a playoff spot in sixteen out of seventeen seasons with Landry leading the way.

During his tenure, he had three outstanding quarterbacks in Meredith, Roger Staubach, and Danny White, and they led the Cowboys through their rise, their ascendant reign, and their decline.

Staubach was the quarterback who helped them win their two Super Bowl titles in the Landry era. He may not have had the arm strength of either Meredith or White, but his superb leadership skills meshed perfectly with Landry's demeanor and innovative ways.

The Cowboys finally won their first Super Bowl following the 1971 season, when they defeated the Miami Dolphins 24–3 in Super Bowl VI. The Cowboys performed almost flawlessly, as they took apart the up-and-coming Dolphins.

The game was a sharp contrast to the previous year's Super Bowl in which the Baltimore Colts had outlasted the Cowboys 16-13 in a game that would become known as the "Blunder Bowl" because the two teams combined for 11 turnovers.

"That game stayed with us throughout the offseason and into training camp," Landry said. "I knew that if we got back to the Super Bowl, we would not see that kind of game again. We got there and we were prepared for the situation."

The Cowboys would win the Super Bowl again following the 1977 season, when Landry's experienced team outclassed the Denver Broncos 27-10. Denver head coach Red Miller had a ferocious defense and an opportunistic offense led by former Dallas quarterback Craig Morton, but there was no way that Landry's defense was going to give the Denver offense a chance to find its rhythm.

The flex defense, designed by Landry during the 1960s, involved his defensive linemen changing their positions—flexing—an instant or two before the ball was snapped. This formation served to confuse quarterbacks who weren't sure which play would work against a defense that they knew would change before the ball was snapped.

That flex defense was instrumental in two more Super Bowl appearances in the 1970s against the Pittsburgh Steelers. The Cowboys would engage Chuck Noll's Steelers in two of the decade's most exciting Super Bowls, and Dallas came up a tad short in both of them.

While they could not defeat the Steelers, there was something heroic about the Cowboys' performances, considering the fact that the Steelers of the '70s would go down as one of the NFL's greatest teams of any era. The Steelers would win four championships in the decade.

Landry kept his emotions in check throughout his career on the sidelines, and that was a conscious decision. There were never any tears following the victories or the defeats. He didn't want to show any form of a perceived weakness, because he knew his players would follow his example.

But in masking his feelings for the majority of his career, he built walls between himself, his players, and his coaches.

Walt Garrison, one of his top running backs in the 1960s and '70s, was once asked if he had ever seen Landry smile. Garrison, always quick with the quip, gave a response that provided great insight into Landry's demeanor.

"No I haven't, but I've only been here nine years," Garrison said.

Keeping emotions and feelings in check was the way many American men conducted themselves at the time. While the strong, silent type is no longer the norm, it worked for Landry as a football coach.

The Cowboys started to lose their way in the 1980s, and they suffered through three consecutive seasons from 1986 through 1988. After the 1988 season, Arkansas oil man Jerry Jones bought the Cowboys. Jones appeared to know that Landry's time had passed.

He replaced him with college coach Jimmy Johnson suddenly and harshly.

The firing was widely criticized because Jones seemed to show no concern for the coach who had led the Cowboys from their first game. He later acknowledged his mistake and admitted that he should not have been so blatant in the move, but he had a plan and was quick to act on it.

Landry was angry and embarrassed, but he did not write a tell-all book, go on television, or try to get even with the owner who forced him out of a job he held for twenty-nine years.

Instead, he went to the Hall of Fame in 1990 having won 250 regular-season games and twenty more in the postseason. Only George Halas and Don Shula won more regular season games, and no coach has ever won more postseason games.

The sight of Landry stalking the sidelines in his trademark fedora remains one of the classic images of the NFL.

For the record

> **Tom Landry**
> Hall of Fame, 1990
> Regular-season record: 250-162-6, .607
> Postseason record: 20-16, .556
> Two Super Bowl victories

#4

DON SHULA

His name is at the top of the list in regular-season and all-time coaching wins. Don Shula might also be at No. 1 in this book if he had been able to handle his postseason business with consistency.

Shula's postseason record is the only area where he comes up short in comparison to coaches like Vince Lombardi, Bill Belichick, and perhaps Tom Landry. However, he ran his teams in the NFL for thirty-three seasons and he picked up 328 regular-season wins and nineteen more in the postseason.

Shula will almost certainly remain at the top of the victory list for the foreseeable and distant future. The idea of any coach lasting thirty-three years seems out of the question at this point, and it took a man of remarkable energy to last that long in the NFL.

Shula played in the NFL from 1951 through 1957 with the Browns, Colts, and Redskins before he began his coaching career at the University of Virginia and the University of Kentucky, respectively. He had his chance to move into the NFL as the defensive coordinator of the Detroit Lions, and he became one of the first coaches to use a zone setup. He helped the Lions build one of the toughest defenses in the NFL.

Carroll Rosenbloom, the owner of the Baltimore Colts, had taken notice of how well Shula had done in Detroit and could sense that he was fine head-coaching timber. While he had Weeb Ewbank on the sidelines, Rosenbloom grew tired of the team's mediocrity, and he fired his coach and replaced him with the thirty-three-year-old Shula.

Shula's first team in Baltimore finished with an 8-6 record in 1963, and the Colts players quickly learned how demanding their new coach was. A winning record was simply not good enough, and Shula let his players know, via his blunt language and fiery temper, that he was not satisfied.

Shula was fierce in his preparations and he worked his players hard. Hall of Fame quarterback Johnny Unitas said Shula made "enemies" out of some of his players because of his hard-driving ways, but they all knew he was an excellent coach.

The Colts came roaring out of the gate in 1964 and finished with a 12-2 record to gain first place in the West Division.

The Colts were heavily favored in the NFL Championship game against the Cleveland Browns, but Unitas & Co. simply could not get it done and they were drummed 27-0.

The Colts were bitterly disappointed with that loss, and they began the 1965 season with new determination. However, they could only tie the Green Bay Packers for first place in the West with a 10-3-1 record, and that meant the two teams had to meet in a playoff game to decide who would meet the Browns in the NFL championship.

Injuries had depleted both teams, and neither Unitas nor backup Gary Cuozzo could play for the Colts. They were forced to have running back Tom Matte play quarterback. The Packers' Bart Starr could not play, and he was replaced by backup Zeke Bratkowski.

It was a brutal war in Green Bay, and the Packers tied the game in the fourth quarter on a late field goal by Don Chandler. That kicker would end the game in overtime on a controversial 25-yard field goal that appeared to be wide of the goalpost, but was called good by the officials.

Shula and the Colts would have to bide their time while the Packers dominated through the mid-1960s, but the Colts put an overpowering team on the field in 1968. Baltimore would roll to a 13-1 record, as they had a ferocious defense led by huge Bubba Smith and nasty middle linebacker Mike Curtis.

The Colts defeated the Minnesota Vikings 24-14 in the divisional playoffs and embarrassed the Browns 34-0 in the NFL Championship game.

That victory gave the Colts the chance to represent the NFL in Super Bowl III against the American Football League's New York Jets.

The AFL had been beaten handily in the first two Super Bowls, and the Colts were an even heavier favorite over the Jets than the Packers had been against the Kansas City Chiefs and Oakland Raiders in the first two AFL-NFL Championship games.

Jets quarterback Joe Namath and his teammates didn't care what the oddsmakers thought and they were confident that they could not only stay with the Colts, but also find a way to beat them. When Namath was goaded by Baltimore fans at a pre-Super Bowl event during the week of the game, he offered his famous "guarantee" that the Jets would win.

Shula and his players were amused and perhaps annoyed with Namath's bold remarks, but they did not change anything in their game plan prior to the game. After all, they had won fifteen of sixteen games and had overpowered the NFL's best teams. Surely, they would steamroll the Jets as well.

But Ewbank's Jets had learned all of the Colts' offensive and defensive schemes, and they came up with the perfect game plan. The Jets intercepted four passes and came up with the biggest upset in the history of pro football with a 16–7 triumph that cloaked the AFL in legitimacy and pride.

Shula and the Colts were shamed by the defeat, and they struggled to an ordinary 8–5–1 record the following year.

Shula left the Colts after that season and moved on to the Miami Dolphins in 1970. Shula built a team that had speed, clutch quarterback play under Bob Griese, and a ferocious and athletic defense.

The Dolphins won the AFC title in 1971, but lost the Super Bowl to the Dallas Cowboys. By the time the Dolphins went to training camp in 1972, they knew they had a tremendous team that was not going to be satisfied unless it won the Super Bowl.

However, while the Dolphins did not appear to have any weaknesses, they went through a significant challenge when Griese was injured early in the season and backup Earl Morrall had to take over.

Morrall ended up starting nine games for Miami, and they won them all. In fact, Miami won every game that season and had a remarkable 14–0–0 mark in the regular season. The Dolphins had a brilliant running game with Larry Csonka, Mercury Morris, and Jim Kiick, and a spectacular "No-Name" defense.

That nickname was given because, although the Dolphins had a star in middle linebacker Nick Buoniconti, the rest of their defense was largely unknown.

By the end of the season, Vern Den Herder, Jake Scott, and Dick Anderson were hardly unknowns.

The Dolphins were spectacular in the regular season and even better in the playoffs. They defeated the Cleveland Browns and the Pittsburgh Steelers to earn the AFC title, and met the NFC's Washington Redskins at the Los Angeles Coliseum in Super Bowl VII.

Despite the Dolphins' perfect record, they were actually one-point underdogs to George Allen's "Over-the-Hill Gang." The Dolphins jumped to a 14-0 lead and held on for a 14-7 team.

It was Shula's first championship, and his team again repeated that winning performance in 1973. While they were not undefeated, the Dolphins may have been even better that year. They earned a 24-7 victory over the Minnesota Vikings in Super Bowl VIII.

That turned out to be Shula's last Super Bowl triumph. His Dolphins remained remarkably consistent for the next twenty-three years, but they never won the Lombardi Trophy again.

Shula proved remarkably adaptable to his personnel. He was viewed as largely a conservative, old-school coach, but when the Dolphins drafted strong-armed Dan Marino in 1983, he opened up the offense and developed one of the best passing games the league had ever seen.

"You have to know the type of players that you have, and give them the best chance to win," Shula said. "It's not about being conservative or wide open. It's about playing to your athletes' strengths."

While Shula's teams were often frustrated in the postseason, no coach ever won more games, and that's why he is one of the most storied coaches in NFL history.

For the record

Don Shula
Hall of Fame, 1997
Regular-season record: 328-156-6, .678
Postseason record: 19-17, .528
Two Super Bowl victories

#5

BILL WALSH

Few coaches have ever taken a team that was at the bottom of the NFL heap and catapulted it to the top more dramatically than Bill Walsh did with the San Francisco 49ers.

Walsh was hired by the 49ers in 1979, after the team had gone 2-14 and was the laughingstock of the NFL. It didn't seem like Walsh would be much of a head coach, as the Niners repeated that 2-14 mark in his first year.

However, there was a huge difference between the 1978 team and the 1979 version. While they did not win any more games, Walsh gave them a game plan and an offensive scheme that would serve the team in an extraordinary manner over the next two decades.

Walsh had prepared to become a head coach by learning from two of the game's masters. His first job as a pro football coach had been with the Oakland Raiders, where he had been the running backs' coach on Al Davis's team. Davis, who had been trained under Sid Gillman, favored the vertical passing game. Walsh learned how Davis wanted to attack quickly and decisively, and he gained the foundation of an offense while with the Raiders.

Walsh would come into his own as an assistant coach with the Cincinnati Bengals from 1968 through 1975. Head coach Paul Brown was clearly one of the game's most innovative coaches, both with the Bengals and prior to that with the Cleveland Browns. Walsh teamed up with Brown to help transform the Bengals from an American Football League expansion team to an NFL winner.

However, when Brown retired prior to the 1975 season, Walsh was passed over for the head coaching job. Brown named Bill "Tiger" Johnson as his successor, and Walsh left the team in a huff.

Brown kept Walsh from getting an NFL head coaching job on numerous occasions after that by giving him lukewarm praise or offering critical comments when other teams called him to ask about Walsh. Brown was one of the most revered men in the NFL, and he was able to keep Walsh from getting ahead in his career. However, he couldn't stop the 49ers from hiring Walsh in 1979.

Walsh was not a typical coach who would work his players to a frazzle in training camp and practice. His philosophy was to build a team that was so skilled and smart that it would be able to run circles around its opponent on Sundays in the regular season.

He believed in concepts like strength, toughness, and physicality, but only to the point where his team was on even terms with opponents. He didn't want to overpower opponents; he wanted his team to have the edge in talent and skill. He was far more interested in winning the chess match with opposing coaches.

This was not an ego-driven goal for Walsh. He simply wanted to take the offensive principles that he had learned and then perfected and build the strongest team possible. He wanted to teach his principles to his players, and have them play at a nearly perfect level on the field.

Walsh would find success in his third year with the 49ers. After his 1980 team went 6-10, few thought the 49ers were ready to become contenders. However, Walsh had a brilliant quarterback in Joe Montana at the helm, and he had engineered a masterful draft that offseason that brought the 49ers four athletic, young defensive backs in Ronnie Lott, Eric Wright, Carlton Williamson, and Lynn Thomas.

Lott would go on to become a Hall of Famer and one of the best safeties in the history of the game, and the young foursome helped turn the Niners into one of the most aggressive defenses in the league.

But it was the offense that allowed this team to make its imprint. Walsh took the best of the offenses that he learned from Gillman, Davis, and Brown and put his own stamp on it to come up with his innovative West Coast Offense.

Instead of merely focusing on the deep ball as Davis had done with his vertical attack, Walsh spread out the defense and hit opponents with a game plan that allowed the Niners to find the weak spots on the flanks.

The key to the attack was having a quarterback who could read defenses expertly and throw the ball accurately. That description fit Montana to a T. He was able to diagnose what the defense was going to do before the snap and adjust his play call, if necessary, to take advantage of it.

The Niners knew they had something special brewing that season when the Dallas Cowboys came to Candlestick Park in Week 6. Walsh's team had a 3-2 record and they knew they were in for a test against Tom Landry's perennial power.

However, in this game, the Niners blew out the Cowboys 45-14. That game gave the 49ers the confidence to know they could play with and beat the best teams in the NFL.

"It was a great moment for us," Lott said. "We had a good mix of young players and veterans and we knew we were getting better. But to beat Dallas like that was a huge step. We all felt good going into that game because we knew we had a great game plan that would keep us in the game. But to blow them out like that had a long-lasting effect."

The 49ers were on a roll after that and would lose only one more game all season. However, they would find themselves right back at Dallas in the NFC Championship game at Candlestick Park.

The Cowboys would claim they overlooked the 49ers in the earlier meeting. That was obviously not the case in the championship game, with a Super Bowl appearance on the line.

The 49ers played well in that game, but the Cowboys had been just a tad better. The 49ers were trailing 27-21 late in the game, when Montana led them on an improbable drive that culminated with the quarterback throwing a game-winning touchdown pass to wide receiver Dwight Clark in the back corner of the endzone that gave San Francisco a 28-27 victory.

"The Catch" signified the rise of the 49ers and the demise of the Cowboys, who would struggle to maintain their elite position after that loss.

Walsh designed that play to give Montana options if he faced pressure. "That was a practiced play," Walsh said. "Now, we didn't expect three guys to be coming right at Joe, but he executed the play to perfection, as he put it, where only Dwight could catch it and nobody could deflect or intercept it."

Walsh had demanding standards for all his players in games and practices, but he also knew when to back off and lighten things up.

When the Niners arrived at the Super Bowl following their dramatic win over the Cowboys, Walsh greeted his players at the hotel in Detroit dressed as a bellman as he helped them with their luggage.

"It may have seemed like a strange thing to do, but Bill always did everything for a reason," Lott said. "He wanted his players to have fun and he wanted to make sure we didn't take it too seriously. He wanted us to relax in the spotlight, and he knew just the right thing to do to take the edge off the situation."

The ploy worked perfectly as the Niners were able to come up with a superb effort as they defeated the Cincinnati Bengals 26-21. It not only gave San Francisco its first NFL championship, but perhaps even more rewarding was the fact that it came against the team that Walsh seemed destined to coach until he had been bypassed.

While Walsh could motivate his team to come up with big emotional efforts, it was his ability to scheme, diagnose, and devise a game plan that made him one of the greatest coaches of all time. He was able to lead the Niners to three Super Bowl titles, and after he retired following the 1988 championship season, former assistant George Seifert led the Niners to two more titles.

Walsh was seemingly at the top of his game following the 1988 season, in which the Niners won the Super Bowl and again defeated the Bengals. But Walsh was no longer enjoying himself and he felt he was having a much harder time reaching his players.

The Niners were just 6–5 shortly after midseason, and they were not playing to their potential. Walsh saw this as an indictment against his coaching style. He was able to rally his team from that point, but he no longer thought he was the best man for the job and he left the Niners.

Walsh would go on to regret the decision. He had high standards for himself and his team, and he didn't understand why his team went through a rare slump. If he had been able to look at the big picture, he could have stayed longer and enjoyed even more success.

He later told the *San Jose Mercury News* that he had made a mistake. "I never should have left," Walsh said. "I'm still disappointed in myself for not continuing. There's no telling how many Super Bowls we could have won had I stayed."

Walsh would go on to try his hand at college coaching (at Stanford University), television analysis, and writing. He would never again reach the heights he had enjoyed with the 49ers.

Walsh's brilliance and talent helped turn a moribund team into one of the glamour franchises in the history of the NFL.

For the record

> **Bill Walsh**
> Hall of Fame, 1993
> Regular-season record: 92-59-1, .609
> Postseason record: 10-4, .714
> Three Super Bowl victories

#6

PAUL BROWN

The New York Jets' victory over the Baltimore Colts in Super Bowl III (see chapter 4, Don Shula) is often viewed as the greatest upset in the history of professional sports. Joe Namath led the upstarts from the American Football League to an upset of the mighty Colts from the NFL, and thereby lifted the AFL and cut the older league down to size.

Well, as dramatic and exciting as that victory was, it was not unprecedented. In 1950, the NFL absorbed four teams from the rival All-American Football Conference, and it was expected that the NFL would trounce the Baltimore Colts, Cleveland Browns,

New York Yanks, and the San Francisco 49ers when they started to compete.

The Browns had been the champions of the AAFC, and they met the defending NFL champion Philadelphia Eagles in the 1950 season opener. However, instead of a one-sided win by the Eagles in front of their home fans, the visiting Browns trounced the Eagles 35-10.

The architect of that Cleveland victory was head coach Paul Brown, who had put together a superb team even though he didn't have the benefit of an NFL affiliation.

What Brown did have was superb coaching skill. Whether it was player evaluation, teaching a system, coaching players individually, or motivating them as a group, Brown was simply an A-plus leader.

Brown excelled as a head coach at all levels of the game. It started at Washington High School in Massillon, Ohio, where he went 80-8-2 and won six straight state championships. Brown moved to Ohio State for a three-year stint and won a national championship with the Buckeyes. After two successful years during the war with the Great Lakes Naval Station football team, Brown was named the coach of the Cleveland franchise in the newly formed AAFC.

Owner Mickey McBride wanted to name the team after his new coach and call it the Browns, but Brown rejected the idea. When the team settled on a nickname of the Panthers, the owner of a defunct franchise that had been called the Cleveland Panthers objected, saying he still had the rights to the name.

McBride didn't want a court fight on his hands, and Brown relented to McBride's original idea, so the team was called the Browns.

Brown built a dominant team in the AAFC. The squad went 52-4-3 in four seasons and won the championship every year. They had a sensational crew of players that included quarterback Otto Graham, fullback Marion Motley, wide receiver Mac Speedie, tackle Lou "The Toe" Groza, guard Alex Agase, and linebacker Lou Saban.

In addition to the talent, Brown was able to get the most out of his players. He did not do it with kindness and love in practice. It was clear that he was the unquestioned boss in every game he ever coached, every practice session he led, and every chalk-talk session he ever presented.

He was not interested in having his players like him, and he was only interested in having them play as he directed. If players made multiple mistakes in practices, Brown would greet them with an icy stare, followed by a sarcastic remark.

Remarkably, Brown would catch nearly every mistake and his players quickly realized they could not fool him at all. As a result, the only conclusion was for them to work diligently so they could do things right and avoid their coach's righteous indignation.

The razor-sharp Brown introduced many aspects of football that became staples in the game. Brown was the first football executive/coach to have a taxi squad of players who were not on the roster, but were ready when called upon.

When it came to giving his quarterback a play, he was the first coach to have a radio installed in his signal-caller's helmet. He was the first coach to grade game films and then go over those films with his players. He also was the first head coach to hire full-time assistant coaches and pay them to work for twelve months a year.

Brown was a master at scouting college players and finding the greatest talent. He introduced rudimentary athletic tests that included the 40-yard dash.

He popularized pocket passing, the draw play, and timed pass patterns that called for the quarterback to throw to a certain spot at a specific count, instead of when the receiver completed his route. This brought football to a new level, and other coaches throughout the league and in the college ranks followed his lead.

He had a finely tuned machine on his hands during the 1950 season. After Brown served notice in the ballyhooed season opener against the Eagles regarding the strength of his team, the Browns rolled throughout the season and finished with a 10-2 record.

They were pushed hard by the New York Giants and the Los Angeles Rams in the postseason, but won both games and earned the NFL championship in their first year in the league.

Brown was never satisfied with merely winning one championship. He wanted to dominate every year. The Browns followed with three seasons that included 11-1, 8-4, and 11-1 records, but they did not win the title in any of those years.

However, the Browns were 9-3 in the 1954 season and won the NFL's East Division title, and that put them in the championship game against the Detroit Lions. Interestingly, the Browns had closed the season with a 14-10 loss to the Lions and another close game was expected.

Nevertheless, Brown had saved something for the title game, and his team overwhelmed the Lions 56-10, as Graham threw three touchdown passes and ran for two more.

The Browns were not done at the close of that season, though. They followed with a 9-2-1 record in 1955 and another championship game appearance. This time they went out to Los Angeles and rolled over the Rams 38-14, after opening the game with a field goal from Groza and a 65-yard interception return for a touchdown from Don Paul. They were never threatened.

After ten seasons of coaching at the professional level, Brown's teams had won seven championships and the worst they had done was 8-4 in any season. He was innovative, clearly a brilliant teacher, and able to inspire his players.

The Browns endured their first losing season in 1956 when they went 5-7, but they bounced back in 1957 after he drafted running back Jim Brown from Syracuse. Jim was a powerful running back who had dominated in college, and Paul Brown made sure his game plan allowed the running back to show off his talents.

The Browns went 9-2-1 in '57 and 9-3 in '58, and made it to the playoffs in both seasons. However, they were stopped by the Lions in the '57 title game and lost to the Giants in the '58 tiebreaker after both teams finished with the same record in the East Division.

The Browns would not make it back to the postseason in any of their four ensuing seasons under Brown, but they did have a winning record every season.

Players, including Jim Brown (who thought his coach's offensive tactics had grown conservative), started to tune out the coach. At about the same time, young businessman Art Modell bought the team, and he wanted to learn more about football by getting inside the mind of his coach.

Brown would have none of it, and he rebuffed Modell's advances even though he owned the team. This went on for a couple of years and Modell eventually fired the coaching legend after the 1962 season.

Brown was out of football until the 1968 season, when he became owner and coach of the Cincinnati Bengals, an AFL expansion team. After two difficult opening seasons, Brown led the Bengals to the playoffs in 1970. The team's quick ascension showed that Brown still had many of his remarkable coaching skills.

He continued to coach the team through the 1975 season, when the sixty-seven-year-old Brown led the team to an 11-3 record.

His legacy should have ended there with great memories, but Brown had grown difficult and small-minded as he got older. He could have turned the Bengals over to assistant coach Bill Walsh, but he thought that Walsh was too eager and he passed him over for the more subservient Bill "Tiger" Johnson.

When Walsh felt the need to strike out on his own with a head coaching position, Brown tried to ruin his efforts by talking him down to every team he could. The 49ers ignored Brown's negative comments and hired Walsh, a move that turned the fortunes of that franchise around.

There was a demeaning edge to Brown's personality that grew in his final years, but it could not take away his remarkable coaching achievements. He had dramatic success at every level of the game, and that's a scenario that no other coach is likely to repeat.

For the record

Paul Brown
Hall of Fame, 1967
Regular-season record: 213-104-9, .672
Postseason record: 9-8, .529
Four AAFC championships, Three NFL championships

#7

BILL PARCELLS

T he Big Tuna cast a big shadow over the game of football, and no coach has ever been so successful with so many teams.

Bill Parcells would have easily been a top-20 head coach if his career had come to an end after he decided to leave the New York Giants following his second Super Bowl victory with them in 1991. But that was not the end of his coaching career, as he would go on to do quite a bit more.

He would also have successful coaching stints with the New England Patriots, New York Jets, and Dallas Cowboys before he would walk away from the sidelines.

Parcells was a New Jersey guy, and he never tried to hide it. In the 1970s, there was a famous television commercial with actor Robert Conrad putting a battery on his shoulder, and looking into the camera for a solid second before he said, "Go ahead, I dare you. Knock it off my shoulder."

Conrad jutted out his jaw in a defiant act of toughness, and sent the message that anyone who tried to knock it off his shoulder was going to have to defend his actions.

Parcells took on much of that same kind of persona in his dealings with the media and, at times, his players. He was a tough guy, and he was going to let everyone know it. Nobody could disrespect Parcells and get away with it.

That was the most famous part of his personality, but it was not the only part. He was thoughtful, honest, and unafraid to change his mind if he thought that would help his team.

That was something he demanded from his assistants, players, and anyone he dealt with. Those who weren't straightforward with Parcells would not be forgiven.

Parcells got his chance to coach in the NFL with the Giants as an assistant on Ray Perkins's staff. During the 1981 season, Parcells was responsible for running the Giants' defense. That was the same season they drafted Lawrence Taylor out of North Carolina, and it was no coincidence that it was the first season that the Giants made it back into the NFL postseason since 1963.

Parcells knew from the first day of training camp that Taylor was special and that he would almost certainly become a game-changing player. He made sure Perkins knew how good Taylor was from the start, and Parcells was instrumental in Taylor becoming a star right from the start of the season.

Parcells would eventually become the Giants' head coach when Ray Perkins left the team to take over for the late Bear Bryant at Alabama. Parcells made mistakes that first year, and the Giants went just 3-12-1. He had a fiery, tough, and resolute personality, but he did not let it show that season.

His job was in jeopardy. Giants' general manager George Young knew ownership was not happy, and he had several conversations with Howard Schnellenberger of the University of Miami. If Schnellenberger had wanted it, he almost certainly could have been head coach of the Giants. That's what Parcells believed.

Schnellenberger did not become head coach of the Giants, and Parcells stayed. He put together a team that was founded on defense, a pounding offensive game plan that featured tough running, and special teams that didn't make mistakes and could force opponents into serious errors.

The Giants became a playoff team in 1984, as they gained a wild-card spot with a 9-7 record and beat the Los Angeles Rams on the road in their first playoff game under Parcells. Although New York lost in the next round to the San Francisco 49ers, Parcells had the core of his team.

In addition to Taylor, the Giants had Leonard Marshall, Carl Banks, Harry Carson, and Jim Burt on defense. Parcells also committed to Phil Simms at quarterback that season, and the move helped steady the offense.

The Giants were 10-6 in 1985 and back in the playoffs once again. This time the 49ers came east to play at Giants Stadium, and the marauding New York defense punished the Niners and shut down their vaunted attack, en route to a 17-3 victory.

Parcells and the Giants were feeling quite confident after the win, and they believed they could continue to advance in the postseason, even though they were going to Chicago to take on the 15-1 Bears. The confidence lasted all the way through kickoff, but once the game started, New York provided little competition for Mike Ditka's team. The Giants simply could not move the ball at all against the Monsters of the Midway and dropped a 21-0 decision on a brutally cold day at Soldier Field.

It was a painful defeat, but it also provided an important lesson for the Giants. They saw how the Bears attacked and dominated on defense, and Parcells got the message across to his players that they had to do the same thing if they were ever going to get to the Super Bowl.

The Giants were a nasty, hard-hitting, take-no-prisoners kind of team in 1986, and it appeared that Parcells message was taken seriously. They roared through the season with a 14-2 record, and appeared to be nearly as good as Chicago had been the year before.

Many were expecting an epic confrontation between the two teams in the NFC Championship game, but the Redskins ended up upsetting the Bears, and that meant Joe Gibbs was bringing Washington to Giants Stadium to decide the NFC Championship.

This time, the Giants would not be stopped. Despite playing in howling winds, the Giants dominated the game from start to finish on both sides of the ball and earned a 17-0 triumph.

That meant a Super Bowl date with the Denver Broncos and John Elway. Many thought the athletic and strong-armed Elway would be the difference in this game, but the Giants would have none of it. After enduring some first-half jitters, the Giants rolled to a 39-20 victory, as Simms completed 22-of-25 passes.

Parcells celebrated with his players, telling them that no matter what happened the rest of their lives, they would always be Super Bowl champions. "They can't take this away from you," he said in the locker room.

Parcells and the Giants would get back to the Super Bowl following the 1990 season. The Giants were 13-3 that year, but they appeared to suffer a crippling blow when Simms went down with a late-season injury. The Giants went into the postseason with backup Jeff Hostetler at quarterback.

Many thought that Hostetler had neither the arm strength nor the leadership ability to lead them past the Bears in the divisional playoffs.

However, New York rolled over Chicago by a 31-3 margin. Then they shocked the 49ers 15-13 the following week to earn a spot in Super Bowl XXV against the high-powered Buffalo Bills.

Buffalo was an offensive juggernaut that year, and they were coming off a monstrous 51-3 blowout over the Los Angeles Raiders in the AFC title game. The Bills were significant favorites to beat the Giants, and even Parcells knew his team did not have the fire-power to keep up with the Bills.

Instead, he told the offensive coordinator to "shorten the game." Parcells didn't just want the Giants to score, but also he wanted them to hold on to the ball, so Jim Kelly and the Buffalo offense were unable to find their rhythm. The Giants had possession for more than forty minutes and pulled out the 20-19 upset when the Bills' kicker sent the potential game-winning field goal wide right.

Parcells left coaching after that win, but he resurfaced with New England in 1993, and he quickly turned that team into a contender. The Patriots won the AFC in 1996, but they lost the Super Bowl to the Green Bay Packers.

Parcells wasn't satisfied in merely serving as the head coach of the Pats. He wanted to have a say in player personnel. This led to a rift with owner Bob Kraft, as Parcells famously made his case: "If you're good enough to cook the food, you're good enough to buy the groceries."

Parcells eventually went on to coach the Jets and Cowboys. He turned around both of those teams, which had struggled before he got there, with his straightforward approach.

Parcells left the sidelines after the 2006 season and moved on to a front-office position with the Miami Dolphins. He ultimately turned that team around before retiring as well.

Overall, he won two Super Bowl titles and left four teams better off than when he arrived.

Not bad for the ultimate Jersey guy.

For the record

Bill Parcells
Hall of Fame, 2013
Regular-season record: 172-130-1, .570
Postseason record: 11-8, .579
Two Super Bowl victories

41

#8

CHUCK NOLL

B.C. has a different meaning in Pittsburgh than it does in the rest of the world.

In the Steel City, B.C. means Before Chuck, because the Pittsburgh Steelers were one of the most forgettable and inconsequential franchises in all of sports before they hired Chuck Noll as head coach in 1969.

But once Chuck Noll came aboard, the Steelers rose from the muck and mire of the NFL's bottom feeders and became perhaps the most glorious team in the NFL.

The Steelers have won six Super Bowl titles, and that's more than any other team in the league. They won the first four of those Super

Bowls under Noll, who found much of the talent that brought glory to Pittsburgh, trained it, and developed the team into the greatest winners the game has known.

The Steelers were a collection of mediocre stumblebums through the 1960s, and they were the type of team that would play aggressively every week but come out on the short end of the scoreboard. Opponents would often pay a price for playing the Steelers, but they would also come away with the win.

Owner Art Rooney was sick of that legacy and when he hired Noll to be his head coach in 1969, he had hope that this single-minded and determined coach would turn things around. "The Old Man" probably couldn't have dreamed how much success Noll would have over the course of his run at the helm of the Steelers from 1969 through 1991.

It wasn't immediate, as the Steelers were a putrid 1-13 in Noll's first season. But the disaster of 1969 was preceded by an event that would help Noll turn around the Steelers. They drafted defensive tackle Joe Greene out of North Texas with the fourth pick in the first round.

Greene would go on to become the foundation of the great Steel Curtain defense and one of the top players in the history of the game. The following year, the Steelers drew a lot of raised eyebrows when they selected Terry Bradshaw with the No. 1 pick overall. Bradshaw appeared to be straight off the set of *Hee Haw*, as he had "country bumpkin" written all over him.

But Bradshaw also had a magnificent arm, and Noll tutored him on the intricacies of the pro game. Bradshaw was often unhappy with Noll over the state of their personal relationship, but they formed one of the most productive partnerships in the history of the game.

Success in the draft would become the heartbeat for the Steelers in the Noll era. The Steelers had what is regularly acknowledged to be the best draft of all time in 1974, when they selected four future

Hall of Famers in Lynn Swann, Jack Lambert, John Stallworth, and Mike Webster.

The Steelers slowly improved in their first three seasons under Noll, but they still finished with a 6-8 record in 1971. However, the team would take a huge step up the ladder in 1972, when they won the AFC Central title with an 11-3 record.

Pittsburgh gained great confidence that season, and their first postseason game was a classic. They engaged in a brutal battle with the Oakland Raiders at a frigid Three Rivers Stadium. They carried a 6-0 lead until late in the fourth quarter, but Raiders quarterback Ken Stabler appeared to steal a win for John Madden and the Raiders when he skated thirty yards down the sidelines to score a touchdown in the final minutes that gave the Raiders a 7-6 lead.

The Raiders knew they were one defensive series away from winning the game and advancing to the AFC Championship game against the Miami Dolphins. The Raiders stopped the Steelers on three consecutive plays. On fourth down, Bradshaw ran for his life to escape the Oakland pass rush before he hurled the ball downfield towards backup running back Frenchy Fuqua. Raiders defensive back Jack Tatum blasted Fuqua and the ball in mid-flight, and it flew backwards.

But the play was not dead. Running back Franco Harris tracked the ball and caught it at his shoe tops while running at full speed. He made it all the way into the endzone and scored on a play known as the "Immaculate Reception."

While the Steelers, in turn, lost the AFC title game to the unde-feated Dolphins, the image of the franchise changed dramatically with the miraculous win over the Raiders. The Steelers became legitimate contenders after that game.

Through those years, Noll was the consummate teacher. How-ever, he wasn't just teaching his players. He was also teaching his coaches to do things in the manner that he demanded. So, if Noll wasn't directly instructing his players, he knew that his assistant coaches were delivering the message properly.

Noll appeared to keep his distance from his players. In the current era, it's common for coaches to be seen getting emotional on the sidelines. They will give their players high fives and often celebrate after a key play or dress down a player who has made a poor play or a mental mistake.

That was never Noll's style. He laid out his expectations for the team in his meetings. He let individual players know what he wanted from them in one-on-one meetings, and if he was disappointed, he let them know behind closed doors.

He kept an even demeanor on the sidelines and thus, just by looking at Noll's face, fans were unable to tell if the Steelers were ahead by 10 points or down by 10.

Noll was not the master of the pregame speech, either. He rarely got emotional when talking to his team, as his usual topic was the specifics of the game plan for that particular week.

However, when the Steelers got ready to face the Raiders in the 1974 AFC Championship game, Noll told his players that Oakland head coach John Madden had said the "two best teams in the league" met the previous week when the Raiders had defeated the Dolphins in the divisional playoffs. He took that as an insult and he wanted his players to do so as well.

Noll's team responded to that salt in the wound by beating the Raiders 24-13 in the Oakland Coliseum, and that allowed the Steelers to go to their first Super Bowl.

They dispatched a powerful and athletic Minnesota Vikings team with relative ease in registering a 16-6 win in Super Bowl IX.

In that game, and three other Super Bowl triumphs, Noll had his team mentally prepared and physically ready. "One thing about Chuck is that he was all business," said Hall of Fame defensive back Mel Blount. "It was a different era back then, as we didn't have the kind of media that followed every move.

"But I don't think it would have mattered because Chuck was so single-minded. He was only interested in getting us ready to play and understanding what the opponent was going to do. He was not interested in showing his hand to anyone else or creating an image. He just wanted to give us a chance to play our best game, and he did that nearly every week."

Noll's Steelers won nine AFC Central titles in addition to their four Super Bowl victories. The Steelers would win 10 or more games for seven out of eight seasons from 1972 through 1979.

Noll may have felt proud of himself in his private moments, but he was never one for self-congratulatory remarks.

"There was a good reason for that," Noll said to me in a 1990 interview. "There was always an opponent coming up and we always had future goals. No matter what game we won, that game was in the past as soon as it was over. You had to prepare for your next opponent. If you took time to say how great you were, there was always somebody ready to outwork you. I couldn't let that happen."

That philosophy allowed Noll to turn a franchise around and help the Steelers become one of the most respected organizations in all of sports.

For the record

Chuck Noll
Hall of Fame, 1993
Regular-season record: 194-143-1, .566
Postseason record: 16-8, .667
Four Super Bowl victories

#9

JOHN MADDEN

To millions of football fans, John Madden was the most memorable of all color commentators that has ever been seen on any NFL broadcast.

To millions of other fans, his Madden football video game is the best recreational video in the history of the medium.

Yes, Madden has proven to be a wildly successful businessman away from the game of football and a supersized personality who thrived for decades on the small screen. However, it's safe to say that none of those other ventures would have amounted to very much had he not been one of the game's greatest coaches.

Madden did not coach a long time—just ten years as the head coach of the Oakland Raiders—but he led with vision, consistency, and a strategic know-how that few coaches have ever matched.

Let's start off with the cold, hard facts. Madden coached the Raiders from 1969 through 1978. Among coaches who led their teams for 100 games or longer, Madden has the best winning percentage (.763) of all time (Vince Lombardi ranks second in that category). His Raiders won the first Super Bowl in the franchise's history, capturing Super Bowl IX with a convincing 32–14 victory over a strong Minnesota Vikings team.

His teams tallied a 103–32–7 record, and the Raiders teams played with a remarkable consistency. Madden excelled at diagnosing his team's strengths and then isolating them against their opponents. His strategic abilities often proved the difference between winning and losing throughout his tenure.

When Madden looked at film of his opponents prior to a game, he would not spend hours and hours trying to get to know his opponents. He looked for their weaknesses, so he could decide how to attack.

If he determined that the Raiders' opponents had problems in coverage, his game plan would feature Daryle Lamonica or Ken Stabler throwing over the top to receivers like Fred Biletnikoff or Cliff Branch. If he thought a team had problems stopping the run, he would have Clarence Davis, Mark van Eeghen, and Pete Banaszak soften them up with interior runs.

It was a simple process and Madden rarely got it wrong.

In addition to his strategic abilities, Madden was one of the best motivators of all time. At the time that he became a head coach in 1969, the head coach was usually a tough-minded disciplinarian who did not accept questions from his players or assistant coaches.

Madden was perhaps the forerunner of the modern coach. He was a great communicator who wanted to know what his players thought, and he was not going to threaten their jobs on a regular basis.

If he had to get tough to get his point across, he would do it. However, that was not the way Madden regularly did his business. He wanted his players to be happy, loose, and relaxed so they could play their best football.

The Raiders did things differently and were known for breaking molds. Madden's coaching style was a perfect match for owner Al Davis's "Just Win, Baby" philosophy.

"That's what it was all about," Madden explained during a 2005 interview. "That's why professionals play football and that's why coaches coach at the pro level—to win. Some guys get caught up in trying to show that they are the boss. I never understood it. We only wanted to win games and championships, and I never thought that yelling at guys was the best way to go about it. I still don't."

Madden's attitude and approach had a lot to do with the Raiders' fun-loving and rambunctious team personality. While other teams had dress codes when they went on the road and lengthy rules, Madden didn't push that on his players. He had two rules: Show up on time and play hard.

If players did that, Madden was happy.

Madden was a sharp assistant coach for the Raiders prior to being named head coach. The Raiders had fallen short in the 1968 AFL Championship game against the New York Jets, and that defeat was impossible for Davis to live with.

He did not think that the team had played its best game under John Rauch, and he fired his coach and brought in Madden to lead the team.

Madden was thirty-three years old at the time, and the youngest head coach in the game by a wide margin. Nevertheless, Madden was comfortable in the job from the start, and the Raiders remained competitive without any hiccups.

The Raiders were 12-1-1 in Madden's first season, and they appeared to be the best team in the AFL by a wide margin. They pummeled the Houston Oilers in the first round of the AFL play-offs, and that set up a meeting with the Kansas City Chiefs in the final AFL Championship game.

The Raiders had beaten the Chiefs in both of their regular-season meetings, and it seemed like they would be able to roll past them in the title game. However, veteran Kansas City coach Hank Stram and quarterback Len Dawson led the defensively sound Chiefs to a 17-7 victory. Kansas City recorded a 23-7 victory over the Vikings in Super Bowl IV, and that moment helped Madden stay focused throughout the rest of his coaching career.

He knew that a successful regular season was a wonderful achievement, but it didn't guarantee anything when a team got to the play-offs. Madden did not measure himself or his team by how many regular-season games the Raiders won. He wanted the championship, and that meant playing their best football in the postseason.

However, the Raiders had two problems. In the early 1970s, Don Shula's Miami Dolphins was the best team in the sport. Shortly after the Dolphins won back-to-back championships, the Pittsburgh Steelers started to assert their dominance.

The Raiders were nearly equal to both teams, but they suffered tough losses to both of those opponents. They lost to the Dolphins in the 1973 AFC Championship game, and they suffered a series of painful defeats to the Steelers in the divisional playoffs or in the conference championship game.

The most famous of those came in 1972, in the so-called "Immaculate Reception" game. The Raiders and Steelers engaged in a brutal defensive struggle on a nasty, cold day in Pittsburgh. The Raiders trailed 6-0 until late in the fourth quarter, when Stabler broke away down the sidelines and scored on a thirty-yard run.

When the Steelers were getting shut down on the next possession, it appeared the Raiders would walk out of Three Rivers Stadium with a 7-6 victory. However, on a fourth-and-long play, Pittsburgh quarterback Terry Bradshaw threw up a miracle—and his prayer was answered. His off-target pass ricocheted off defensive back Jack Tatum (and perhaps off Pittsburgh's John "Frenchy" Fuqua), and into the arms of Franco Harris.

The Steelers running back caught the ball off of his shoe tops and somehow raced into the endzone for the game-winning score.

It took nearly twenty minutes for the officials to determine that Harris's touchdown was legitimate, and many believed that only happened because they thought their lives would be at risk if they reversed the touchdown.

It was a defeat that Madden never got over.

But while that loss seared his soul and remained in his heart, Madden's team continued to win. They finally reached their peak during the 1976 season, when they were overpowering in building a 13-1 record.

Madden wasn't overly impressed with his team's regular-season record, but when they defeated the New England Patriots 24-21 in the divisional playoffs—a controversial win that went the Raiders' way—and the Steelers in the AFC title game, they had earned a spot in the Super Bowl.

It would be the team's first trip to the big game since Super Bowl II, and Madden knew his team was not going to let the opportunity pass.

They had beaten the Steelers on the biggest stage, and while Bud Grant had a fine team in Minnesota and a Hall of Fame quarterback in Fran Tarkenton, the Vikings were simply no match.

The Raiders' offensive line, led by Gene Upshaw and Art Shell, simply obliterated Minnesota's famous Purple People Eaters. The Raiders ran the ball with ease, made big plays through the air, and dominated on defense.

It was Madden's crowning moment.

"That's what you live for as a coach," Madden said. "You have a team, you know your goal, and you go out and achieve it against the best competition in the world. There could not be a better feeling in your professional life."

Madden coached two more seasons before deciding to retire. He had taken his team to the mountaintop, and he would leave the sidelines.

Madden broadcasted the game for far longer than he had coached, but there's no doubt that he was one of the game's greats during the ten years he roamed the sidelines for the Raiders.

For the record

> **John Madden**
> Hall of Fame, 2006
> Regular-season record: 103–32–7, .763
> Postseason record: 9–7, .563
> One Super Bowl victory

#10

GEORGE HALAS

No individual had more to do with the existence and growth of professional football than George Stanley Halas did.

Halas was one of the founding members of the American Professional Football Association, and he was at the initial meeting at Ralph Hay's Hupmobile showroom in Canton, Ohio in 1920. From that point on, Halas either made or was involved in every key decision concerning the National Football League for the next forty-seven years.

Halas started with the Decatur Staleys in 1920, and the team moved to Chicago a year later. By 1922, the team was called the

Bears, and Halas had a number of partners until 1932, when he acquired complete ownership of the team.

Halas had four different coaching stints with the Bears, and each of them was quite successful. He coached them from 1920 through 1929, and stepped down that year when arguments with his partner Dutch Sternaman grew so frequent that he agreed to step aside from his coaching duties until they could be worked out.

Halas's teams had nine winning seasons in their first ten years, and they won their only championship of that decade in 1921.

After Halas gained full control of the team, he returned to the sidelines in 1933. He coached another ten years, and his teams won NFL championships in 1933, '40, and '41. All of those seasons were winning ones for the Bears, but he left the team after five games of the 1942 season because he went into the Navy.

He did not return until the 1946 season, and this time he remained coach through 1955, another ten-year stint. The Bears won their fifth championship under Halas in his first season back, but he endured back-to-back losing seasons in 1952 and '53.

Halas had gotten the Bears back on a winning track in 1954 and '55, but he felt it was time to step down after that season. Paddy Driscoll was his successor, and Halas saw the Bears reach the NFL Championship game in 1956 from afar, but they lost the title. When the Bears endured a losing season in 1957, Halas couldn't take being away from coaching the team any longer and returned to the sidelines.

He had one more ten-year stint, as he coached the team from 1958 through the 1967 season. Halas and the Bears would win a sixth title in 1963, and that would be his last hurrah as a head coach.

But while forty years of being a head coach in the NFL is an overwhelming legacy by itself, there is so much more to this man who had a hand in so many key decisions for the NFL.

His two most memorable championship teams came in 1940 and 1963. In 1939, he brought in Clark Shaughnessy to upgrade the Bears' offense, which had grown stale. He also acquired Sid Luckman to play quarterback for the Bears.

The combination of Halas, Shaughnessy, and Luckman turned out to be a brilliant one, as the Bears went 8-3-0 and won the NFL's West Division, finishing 1 ½ games ahead of the Green Bay Packers. Their last loss of the regular season had been a 7-3 defeat at the hands of the Washington Redskins.

Washington went 9-2 and won the East Division, and they appeared to be the better team when they met in Griffith Stadium for the NFL Championship. But the Bears had a surprise in store for the Redskins, as they eschewed their old single-wing formation and came out with the T-formation.

The Redskins were bollixed and confused on the defensive end and the Bears ran roughshod over them in a 73-0 victory. That remains the most one-sided triumph in NFL and championship game history.

Ten players combined for eleven touchdowns that day, as Halas and the Bears ushered the NFL into the modern era.

Halas had put together a defensive juggernaut in the early 1960s. The Bears had finished third in the West Division in 1962 with a 9-5 record, behind the 13-1 Green Bay Packers and the 11-3 Detroit Lions. Halas knew his team had a difficult assignment in front of them, because the Packers won the championship that year and there were no signs of weakness.

But the Bears had a defense that featured Doug Atkins, Bill George, and Ed O'Bradovich and an excellent supporting cast that took pleasure in not only stopping their opponents, but also pounding them unmercifully. The offense could not match the defense's intensity, but tight end Mike Ditka and wideout Johnny Morris gave them enough firepower to be a threat.

The Bears went 11-1-2 in '63, as they beat the Packers twice and took the division by ½ game over their rivals. Their only loss came at San Francisco in Week 6, and they had back-to-back ties in Weeks 11 and 12 against the Pittsburgh Steelers and Minnesota Vikings.

When they hosted the Giants in the NFL Championship game at Wrigley Field on a four-degree day, the Bears were in top form. The Giants opened the scoring on a fourteen-yard touchdown pass from Y. A. Tittle to Frank Gifford, but the Bears stopped New York from reaching the end zone after that and got two rushing touchdowns from quarterback Bill Wade to pull out a 14-10 win.

Halas still had energy after that win, but his team could not keep up with Vince Lombardi's Packers after that. Halas finally decided to call an end to his forty-year coaching career when he got angry at the officials in his last season.

Halas was known for his feisty attitude and cantankerous demeanor. Ditka, after a failed contract negotiation with Halas, said he "threw nickels around as if they were manhole covers."

But while Halas may have been frugal in his negotiations, he was a man who took care of his old friends and teammates, and was incredibly charitable.

Halas was more of a protector than a catalyst for NFL growth. He abhorred the idea of expansion, because that meant that more competitors would get more of a share of the NFL's income, and he never wanted to cut any more pieces of pie.

However, when the American Football League formed, he finally relented on expansion because the new league would have been able to command cities that the NFL wanted for itself.

Halas loved to say no to many proposals and ideas, but he did give his stamp of approval to Pete Rozelle when the league chose the brash public relations guru to be its commissioner in 1960. Rozelle, to his credit, never gave in to Halas after he became commissioner, and his strength in standing up to Halas won him respect around the league, and begrudgingly, from Halas.

Halas had many coaching rivals over the years, but his two most notable rivals were Curly Lambeau and Vince Lombardi in Green Bay.

Halas and Lambeau feuded famously, but despite their personal animus, Halas was instrumental in helping Lambeau get funding for City Field in Green Bay.

On the other hand, Halas loved and respected Lombardi, and the two embraced regularly after games and at league functions.

Lombardi said the only man who he called coach was Halas.

Halas ran the Bears after his coaching days ended, but when his son George "Mugs" Halas Jr. died of a heart attack in 1979, it was a brutal blow for Halas. He had wanted his son to take over for him.

Halas remained in control of the Bears until he died in 1983. One of his last major acts was to hire Ditka as his head coach, and it was a move that would help the Bears win their only Super Bowl following the 1985 season.

Although he passed away more than three decades ago, Halas's imprint remains all over the franchise and the NFL. He is truly one of the most influential figures in the history of North American professional sports.

For the record

George Halas
Hall of Fame, 1963
Regular-season record: 318–148–31, .682
Postseason record: 6–3, .667
Six NFL championships

#11

TOM COUGHLIN

There is little doubt that Tom Coughlin has both the credentials and the longevity to have earned a spot as one of the top coaches the NFL has ever seen.

But even more compelling than his achievements—he took a second-year expansion team to the AFC Championship game and he has won two Super Bowls with the New York Giants—is the personality change that Coughlin went through that allowed him to connect with his players.

That connection was likely the key that helped the Giants go from a talented team that tended to fade in key games to one that played its best football in the most important games.

Coughlin had started his coaching career as a college assistant and had made his most important stops at Syracuse and Boston College. During his time at Boston College, he had helped develop Doug Flutie into one of the most dangerous and charismatic quarterbacks in the nation.

That performance helped Coughlin earn a job as an assistant on the Philadelphia Eagles staff, but the players there did not embrace him. Coughlin was a demanding assistant who made sure that the athletes did things the right way on the practice field and never cut corners. Veterans referred to him as "Technical Tom," and they were relieved when he left Philadelphia after his second season in 1985 and moved on to Green Bay.

After two years with the Packers, Coughlin was hired by Bill Parcells, and he played a key role as the Giants won Super Bowl XXV over Buffalo following the 1990 season. Coughlin went on to become head coach at Boston College, and he helped turn the Eagles into a winning program.

Meanwhile, the Giants wanted Coughlin back as their head coach. Parcells had left the team in 1991 due to health concerns, and the Giants were unhappy with Ray Handley at head coach. They fired Handley and asked Coughlin to take his position, but he remained at Boston College for another year.

Then, when the NFL expanded to Jacksonville in 1995, Coughlin became the Jaguars' first head coach. It was expected that the Jaguars would follow the pattern of most expansion teams and suffer for several seasons with losing records and ill-equipped players, but Coughlin was not willing to go that route.

He gave many unproven veterans a chance to show that they could play, he drafted wisely, and he crafted a resourceful team. The Jaguars went 4-12 that first season, but they were ready to win games the following year.

Inexplicably, the Jaguars went 9-7 that season and earned a spot in the playoffs as an AFC wild-card team. They came into the playoffs with a five-game regular-season winning streak, and while that was impressive, few expected anything but a blowout when they went to Buffalo for their first playoff game.

The Jaguars fell behind by 7-0 and 14-7 margins, but the combination of quarterback Mark Brunell's passing and Natrone Means's running allowed the Jaguars to hang in with the Bills and they eventually pulled out a 30-27 victory.

The Jaguars were undaunted, and the coach pushed his team even harder as they went to Denver to take on the heavily favored Broncos. The Jaguars would fall behind by two touchdowns, but there was no give-up. The Jaguars roared back and shocked the Broncos by another 30-27 margin.

While the Jags were stopped by the Patriots in the AFC Championship game, based on the team's success, Coughlin had demonstrated that he was a formidable NFL.

Jacksonville would win eleven or more games during the next three seasons and get back to the AFC Championship game in 1999 after going a remarkable 14-2. However, they lost that title game to the Titans, and that was the end of Coughlin's hopes of getting to the Super Bowl with the Jaguars, who faded badly over the next three seasons, when the team's talent level diminished and players started to tune out their demanding coach.

Coughlin's run in Jacksonville came to an end with a 6-10 season in 2002, but he was rested and recharged when the Giants came back to him in 2004. New York had a talented team, but the Giants had been undisciplined under Jim Fassel. Coughlin quickly changed that with his hard-nosed rules and militaristic manner.

After a 6-10 season in his first year with the Giants in 2004, he turned things around quickly and they won the NFC East with an 11-5 record in 2005. They appeared to be in position for a decent playoff run, but the Giants were flat and were shut out at home by the Carolina Panthers 23-0.

The following season, the Giants slipped to 8-8, but they still managed to get into the playoffs and they were once again beaten in the first round. Coughlin's approach was wearing thin on a lot of key players and while most tried to keep their differences in house, veteran running back Tiki Barber made no attempt to hide his displeasure with the demanding coach.

While Coughlin initially dug his heels in when he got wind of the players' displeasure, a one-on-one conversation with Giants defensive end and leader Michael Strahan helped Coughlin relate to the players. Strahan urged Coughlin to show a more human side, and the plea worked during the 2007 season.

The Giants came together as the season progressed and they made the playoffs again as a wild-card team. But this time, they were energized as the postseason got underway and they reeled off road wins over Tampa Bay and Dallas to earn a spot in the NFC Championship game against the Packers.

Few expected the Giants to survive a game against Brett Favre in bitterly cold and brutal wind-chill conditions, but the Giants hung in there and forced the game into overtime. Coughlin resembled an icicle as the game concluded with New York placekicker Lawrence Tynes drilling a 47-yard field goal to win the game.

Coughlin had finally taken his team to the Super Bowl, and he had survived frozen Hell to get a shot at the undefeated New England Patriots. The Patriots were playing for a place in history as only the second undefeated World Champions of the Super Bowl era, and they had defeated the Giants in the regular-season finale that year.

But New York conceded nothing to Bill Belichick's Patriots, and the Giants trailed just 14-10 in the fourth quarter. They came through on their final drive, thanks to a spectacular throw and catch from Eli Manning to David Tyree, and the Giants upset the Pats 17-14 when Manning concluded the come-from-behind effort with a touchdown pass to angular wideout Plaxico Burress.

Four years later, the Giants and the Patriots met in the Super Bowl again, and New England remained the heavy favorite. The Giants played harsh defense and held New England in check throughout, and that allowed Coughlin and his players to come away with a 21–17 victory.

Strahan retired shortly after the first Super Bowl win over the Patriots, and he said Coughlin's personality change was the key reason for the success. "Sometimes people change a little bit here and there," Strahan said. "That's pretty much what I expected with Tom. But it was a dramatic change and he showed the players a completely different side, and it had a huge impact on his players."

Coughlin always understood how to formulate a game plan and what kind of attributes players needed to be successful. But until he could reach and relate to his players on an emotional level, he had no chance of being successful. Once that changed, the Giants won two Super Bowls.

They proved to be incredible road warriors, playing only one home game in those two championship runs.

Coughlin has remained head coach of the Giants through this book's printing (mid-2015). Though things have not gone as well for the Giants since their second victory over the Pats, Coughlin's legacy has nevertheless been fulfilled by his 2-0 record in the Super Bowl.

For the record

Tom Coughlin
Regular-season record: 164–140–0, .539
Postseason record: 12–7, .632
Two Super Bowl victories

#12

TONY DUNGY

For years, Tony Dungy appeared to be waiting for his opportunity to become head coach of an NFL team.

He served a long apprenticeship, becoming the youngest assistant coach in the league when he was hired by Chuck Noll as defensive backs coach for the Steelers in 1981. Dungy was able to rise to the defensive coordinator position within three years.

He later coached defensive backs for Marty Schottenheimer in Kansas City and then went with Dennis Green to Minnesota, where he was the defensive coordinator.

It seemed that Dungy was regularly mentioned as the top head coaching candidate among assistants who were looking to take that step up, but he often had a hard time getting interviews or serious consideration. Race appeared to be a factor, because every spot where Dungy had coached, players and other coaches marveled at his demeanor, preparation, communication ability, and teaching talent.

Eventually, Dungy got his opportunity to become a head coach when he was hired by the Tampa Bay Bucs in 1996. At that point, Tampa was a woeful organization. Prior to hiring Dungy, they had lost ten or more games in twelve of their previous thirteen seasons.

The first year was a difficult one for Dungy, as he had been anointed by the fans and media as something of a miracle worker when he took the job since so many of his coaching associates and former players had so many glowing things to say about him.

However, there were no miracles when he took the job with the Bucs. Dungy had a plan for the team to improve, but it did not include any quick fixes.

His team lost its first five games in 1996 before beating the Vikings for their first victory, but then lost three more games in a row to fall to 1–8. The last of those games was against the Chicago Bears. The Bucs dropped a 13–10 decision in Chicago even though they outplayed the Bears from a statistical point of view, and after the game the media surrounded Dungy in the cramped and steamy Soldier Field locker room.

Question after accusatory question was hurled at Dungy, and he handled each and every one of them in a calm and thoughtful manner. It was a situation that almost certainly would have caused many coaches to crack and get explosively angry, but Dungy knew what he was doing and he was not going to let a few setbacks upset him.

That calm demeanor started to rub off on his team, as the Bucs started to play much more efficient and mistake-free football. After that miserable start, the Bucs went 5–2 to close the season and served notice that their days of losing ten or more games every year were over.

The following season, the Bucs went 10-6 in the NFC Central and earned a spot in the playoffs as an NFC wild-card team. The Bucs beat the Lions 20-10 in the playoff game and held Detroit running back Barry Sanders in check.

The newly confident Bucs had designs on playing for the NFC Championship, but those dreams went out the window when Tampa Bay suffered a 21-7 loss at Green Bay in the divisional playoffs. The Packers would go on to beat the Carolina Panthers in the NFC Championship game and the New England Patriots in the Super Bowl.

Dungy had built a formidable defense with the Bucs in just two seasons, and they were regarded as perhaps Green Bay's most legitimate challenger. Players like Warren Sapp, Derrick Brooks, Hardy Nickerson, John Lynch, and Brad Culpepper had given the Bucs' defense a nasty edge that had been missing for years.

The Bucs slipped a bit in 1998, but they were a playoff team for the next three years. They lost in the 1999 NFC Championship game to the St. Louis Rams in a game that they nearly stole away from the eventual Super Bowl champions.

However, they lost to the Philadelphia Eagles in the wild-card round in each of the next two seasons because the Tampa Bay offense had not made any progress. While Dungy had turned the Bucs around overall, he made no progress with their offensive players. He was fired after the 2001 season.

It didn't take long for the Indianapolis Colts to come calling and hire him as head coach. On paper, it seemed like a match that would work well.

Dungy was a proven master at teaching and implementing strong defensive game plans. The Colts already had one of the game's best quarterbacks in Peyton Manning, and their offense was prolific. All Dungy had to do was improve the defense and let the offense take care of itself. If he could do that, the Colts would be a perennial championship contender.

Life is never that simple in the NFL. At the very least, the competition is always making moves to get better, and Dungy found the competition to be formidable in the AFC.

The Colts had no easy path to the Super Bowl. Instead, they found worthy rivals and nasty opponents in Bill Belichick, Tom Brady, and the New England Patriots.

The Patriots would prove to be difficult roadblocks for Dungy, Manning, and the Colts. Indianapolis would make the playoffs and win ten or more games in each of Dungy's first four seasons at the helm of the Colts. However, they lost to the Patriots in the AFC Championship game in 2003 and the divisional playoffs in 2004.

The Pittsburgh Steelers stopped the Colts in the divisional playoffs in 2005, and there was a belief in Indianapolis that Dungy and Manning would never make it to the Super Bowl together, as a duo.

The 2006 season had a much different feel for the Colts, as they came roaring out of the gate with seven straight wins. They went to New England in Week 8, and it seemed likely that their winning streak would come to an end in Foxboro against their archrivals. However, the Colts played a sensational game and defeated the Patriots 27-20 behind a 326-yard, two-touchdown effort from Manning.

The win gave the Colts the confidence they had been missing. As the Colts were enjoying their breakthrough season, Dungy went through the worst kind of personal crisis, as his oldest son committed suicide.

While nothing prepares any parent for that type of brutal pain, Dungy remained calm and in control, thanks to his spiritual and religious convictions.

He remained on the sidelines for the rest of the season, and the Colts defeated the Chiefs and Baltimore Ravens in the playoffs. A trip to the Super Bowl loomed if they could repeat their regular-season success and defeat the Patriots.

It looked like the season would once again end in heartbreak, as the Patriots built a 21-3 second-quarter lead. However, the Colts were undaunted as they came roaring back behind Manning's 349 total passing yards and ultimately secured a 38-34 win.

The Colts were going to the Super Bowl, where they would meet the Chicago Bears, who were coached by Dungy's former assistant Lovie Smith.

The two men were the first African-American coaches to lead their teams to the Super Bowl, and Dungy would get the best of his former student, as the Colts rolled to a 29-17 victory.

The win was the culmination of a sensational coaching career for Dungy. He coached the Colts to a 13-3 record in 2007 and a 12-4 mark in 2008, but they lost in the first round of the playoffs each time.

Dungy decided to retire after that '08 season. Dungy was an NFL head coach for thirteen years, went to the playoffs eleven times, and had just one losing season.

Dungy exhibited a serene confidence from the first day he stepped on the field to the last, and he always treated his players and fellow coaches with respect.

That peaceful strength became his legacy and helped make him one of the game's winningest coaches of all time.

For the record

Tony Dungy
Regular-season record: 139-69-0, .668
Postseason record: 9-10, .474
One Super Bowl victory

#13

SID GILLMAN

The fast-paced, high-powered passing game that is featured in today's NFL started in the fertile mind of Sid Gillman.

The Hall of Famer made a name for himself as the head coach of the powerful San Diego Chargers in the American Football League in the early 1960s, but the ideas for his high-powered, vertical passing game came when he was an end at Ohio State in the 1930s.

Francis "Close the Gates of Mercy" Schmidt was coaching the Buckeyes at the time, and he brought an explosive offense to Columbus. Once Gillman was done with his playing career, he decided to work with Schmidt as an assistant.

That's where Gillman developed his coaching ideas, and after working as an assistant coach at the University of Miami (Ohio) and Army, he got the chance to serve as head coach at the University of Cincinnati. He installed a highly evolved Split-T offense, and the Bearcats went 50-13-2 under Gillman.

The NFL took notice, and the Los Angeles Rams hired him as head coach in 1955. He brought them to the championship game against the Cleveland Browns in his first year, but his team suffered a 38-14 trouncing and never made it back to the championship game again, in his five-year tenure.

Gillman's 1958 team went 8-4, but he had a problem getting his message across to his players. Gillman was not very diplomatic in those days, and his personality rubbed many of his players the wrong way. He was very blunt with them, and Hall of Fame wide receiver Tom Fears criticized him for not getting his players to play hard for him, and accused him of "tearing down the franchise."

The Rams went 2-10 in 1959, and he was fired after that season.

But Gillman was able to get back on the horse quickly, because the American Football League went from Lamar Hunt's drawing board to an actual entity in 1960. Gillman accepted a head coaching job offer from the Los Angeles Chargers.

Gillman put all of his offensive theories into fruition with the Chargers, who would move to San Diego after one year in Los Angeles.

The Chargers were an early powerhouse in the wide-open league, winning the West Division in each of the AFL's first two seasons, but falling short in the championship game both times at the hands of the Houston Oilers.

The Chargers fell badly in 1962 and had a miserable 4-10 season, but Gillman was undaunted. He put together one of the best offensive teams of the 1960s the following year with Tobin Rote at quarterback, Paul Lowe and Keith Lincoln at running back, and the spectacular Lance Alworth at the wide receiver position.

The Chargers went 11–3 that season and scored 399 points during their fourteen-game season. They went into the AFL title game with full confidence against a Boston Patriots team that won the East Division with a 7-6-1 record after they beat the Buffalo Bills in a playoff game.

The Patriots simply did not have the weapons to compete with the Chargers, and San Diego rolled to a 51-10 win for the only title in the team's history.

At that point, the NFL barely recognized the AFL as anything but an annoyance, and the thought of the Chargers getting a chance to compete with the NFL champion Chicago Bears was not any consideration by NFL commissioner Pete Rozelle.

However, Gillman asked Rozelle for a chance to let his team play the Bears by sending him a telegram. Rozelle sent him a condescending dismissal.

That response helped solidify the AFL's competitive fire. From that point forward, the four-year-old league stopped thinking of itself as second-class and wanted to wage war against the NFL. That effort eventually paid off when the two leagues agreed to merge in 1966. The first championship game was played in 1967, and the AFL would play through the 1969 season before the NFL absorbed the AFL teams and divided into two conferences.

Many point to that '63 championship team that Gillman built as the igniter for the AFL's growth and ability to force the NFL's hand just a few years later.

Gillman's Chargers remained a strong team in the AFL after that, but they were eventually bypassed in the West by Al Davis's Oakland Raiders and Hank Stram's Kansas City Chiefs. The Chargers were equal to or better than the Raiders and Chiefs on offense, but they fell short on defense, and that's why they could not win another title game.

They made it back to the AFL Championship game in '64 and '65, but lost to the Buffalo Bills on both occasions. Jack Kemp, who got his start with the Chargers, led the Bills at quarterback, but Gillman eventually decided to go with Rote and the strong-armed John Hadl at quarterback.

Gillman seemed to be more obsessed with building an explosive and artistic offense than he was with winning championships, and that was his undoing. He would coach the Chargers intently, cutting a striking figure with his trademark bow ties on the sidelines.

Gillman had to leave the Chargers in 1969 due to a severe bout with ulcers, and he couldn't return to the team and reclaim his place as head coach until 1971. However, he did not have a hero's welcome when he returned. The Chargers were a mediocre football team at that point, and Gillman had a number of battles with team owner Gene Klein.

Gillman resigned after the first ten games of the season, and he left the team with a 4-6 record. The Chargers went into a tailspin shortly thereafter and struggled badly after he departed.

Still, he was one of the most respected strategists in professional football. Shortly after he left the Chargers, Tom Landry hired Gillman to be his quality control coach. The idea was that Gillman would study film and give Landry his game-plan suggestions based on the Cowboys' strengths and their opponents' weaknesses.

It didn't last long, and Gillman eventually became head coach of the Houston Oilers in 1973 and '74. The Oilers were an awful team when he took over four games into the 1973 season and went 1-9, but he was named coach of the year when he led that team to a 7-7 record the following season.

He stepped down after that, but remained in the game as an advisor and assistant coach at both the college and professional levels.

Gillman probably would not have thrived in the modern era when the bright lights of television and the media would have tracked his every step. He did not like to reveal much of his personality, other than the fact that he was obsessed by the game of football.

His ability to innovate on offense remained his passion for the remainder of his life. Gillman died in 2003, at the age of ninety-one.

For the record

> **Sid Gillman**
> Hall of Fame, 1983
> Regular-season record: 122-99-7, .552
> Postseason record: 1-5-0, .167
> One AFL Championship

#14

JIMMY JOHNSON

Few coaches ever came into the NFL with more hype and hoopla than Jimmy Johnson did when he made his NFL debut in the 1989 season with the Dallas Cowboys.

All Johnson did was replace Tom Landry, who had coached every game for the Dallas Cowboys from their first season in 1960 through 1988. However, when Cowboys owner Bum Bright found himself in financial difficulties and put his team up for sale in 1989, he found an enthusiastic buyer in Jerry Jones.

Jones was an Arkansas-based oil millionaire, and he had dreamed of owning an NFL franchise. Once he got the keys to the car, he was not going to stand on ceremony and slowly warm to the task. He put his imprint on the Cowboys with the boldest possible move.

He fired Landry and he brought in Johnson as his head coach. The move was one that almost certainly had to be made because the Cowboys had grown stale in the final years of the Landry regime. However, Jones came across like an arrogant rube because of the callous way he dismissed Landry.

While the Cowboys had lost their way through the 1980s and it seemed clear that a change at the top was a good idea, Landry was one of the greatest coaches in NFL history and he deserved a bit of dignity.

Jones did not give it to him, and he was taken to task for that. One thing that Jones could not have been accused of was duplicity. He was direct in his approach and decisive in his move.

Johnson had been a top-level college coach at Oklahoma State, and that stint had prepared him for a run at national powerhouse Miami. He coached the Hurricanes to a national championship and the No. 2 position on two other occasions.

Johnson had also been a teammate of Jones when the two played college football together at Arkansas during the 1960s. The perception was that Jones hired his best buddy from college and they were going to attempt to turn the Cowboys back into an NFL power.

Johnson would do just that, but his level of friendship with Jones was greatly overstated. While they were tremendous "buddies" whenever they were on camera together, Jones's ingratiating nature tended to rub Johnson the wrong way. But the working relationship was a good one, and they brought the Cowboys back to prominence.

It wasn't an easy journey, as Johnson's first season in Dallas was a 1-15 disaster. But Johnson had a plan, and he was able to execute it when he was able to commandeer a trade with the Minnesota Vikings.

Jimmy Johnson

Early in that first season, he knew he had a team that wasn't going anywhere because the Cowboys didn't have enough good players who could contribute. However, they did have one brilliant asset in running back Herschel Walker, and Johnson knew that if he traded Walker he could get the kind of players who would help the Cowboys begin to climb up the NFL ladder.

He didn't know how much he could get for Walker, but he found a willing trade partner in Minnesota general manager Mike Lynn. Johnson made a complicated deal that involved trading Walker and several mid-to-late-round picks for Minnesota's first-round pick, six players, and six conditional draft picks.

When Johnson started waiving the players he acquired from Minnesota, that activated those conditional picks into actual draft picks. Johnson continued to move his picks on draft day, and eventually worked deals with fifteen different teams.

The Cowboys were able to remake their roster with talented young players. They already had wide receiver Michael Irvin, and Johnson was able to draft quarterback Troy Aikman and running back Emmitt Smith, and those "triplets" became the cornerstone of the Dallas offense.

The Cowboys made significant progress in 1990 when they nearly reached the .500 mark (7-9). NFC East opponents could see how strong the Cowboys were becoming and that they were going to be difficult to contend with in the years ahead.

The Cowboys made the playoffs as a wild-card team in 1991 with an 11-5 record, and won a playoff game against the Chicago Bears before they were defeated 38-6 by the Detroit Lions in the divisional playoffs.

That defeat steeled the Cowboys for a hard push from their head coach the next season. Johnson was a demanding task master who wanted to get the most out of his young, championship-caliber team. He threatened to bench or cut players any time he did not see a top effort being given on the field, and he carried out those threats without exception.

The Cowboys went 13-3, won the NFC East title, and were the odds-on favorite to roll through the playoffs. But Johnson was anything but a happy man. When his team lost a 20-17 late-season decision to the Redskins in Washington, Johnson ordered all his players to remain in their seats on the flight home and told the flight attendants not to serve food to any of his players.

His explosive temper was on display, and he did not want anyone to take their position on the team for granted. Two weeks later, the Cowboys closed the season with a 27-13 victory over Chicago, but the win was tarnished by sloppy play down the stretch that included two fumbles by backup running back Curvin Richards.

Richards was a talented athlete, but he had major issues holding onto the ball. Of all the sins a player could commit, Johnson thought nothing was worse than fumbling.

He was beside himself with anger after the game, and he cut Richards the next day. While that move was viewed as harsh from the outside, it helped Johnson make sure everyone on the team knew he was serious.

He was not impressed by a 13-3 record or a division title. He wanted a team that functioned smoothly and efficiently at all times, and he was not going to tolerate needless errors.

The Cowboys rolled by the Eagles in the divisional playoffs and beat the San Francisco 49ers 30-20 in the NFC Championship on the road.

That victory earned them a spot in Super Bowl XXVII at the Rose Bowl against the AFC Champion Buffalo Bills. Johnson knew he had the better team during Super Bowl week and that his players were superbly prepared for a maximum effort.

The normally high-strung Johnson was remarkably calm before the game, as his confidence was unshakable. Dallas pummeled the Bills by a 52-17 margin.

The Cowboys were nearly as good the following year and they once again beat Buffalo in the Super Bowl. While they were not quite as dominant as the year before, their 30-13 victory left little doubt that the Cowboys were the superior team.

The Cowboys were a dynasty, but when Jones tried to share the credit with Johnson, he was rebuffed and insulted by his coach. That was more than Jones could bear, and neither man could stomach working with the other any longer.

Johnson left the Cowboys "by mutual decision" and the Cowboys hired former Oklahoma coach Barry Switzer to take over.

The Cowboys eventually won a Super Bowl following the 1995 season under Switzer, but he received almost no credit for it because Johnson had left him with such a powerful roster.

Johnson returned to the NFL in 1996 and coached four more years with the Miami Dolphins, but he was unable to build a juggernaut in Miami.

Though he had a good team, his final game was a 62-7 playoff defeat to the Jacksonville Jaguars. It was an ignominious ending to a brilliant and tempestuous coaching career.

Johnson was more than happy to fade into the sunset, fishing in his boat off the Florida Keys and serving as an NFL analyst for the Fox network.

For the record

Jimmy Johnson
Regular-season record: 80-64-0, .566
Postseason record: 9-4, .692
Two Super Bowl victories

#15

MARV LEVY

The words have become his calling card. When Marv Levy was the coach of the Buffalo Bills, he would gather his team in the locker room, and look each of his players in the eye before a big game.

"Where else would you rather be, than right here and right now?" Levy would say, and those words would inevitably leave his team in a fired-up state.

But in many ways, Levy was an atypical head coach. He did not rule by fear and he was not known for his locker room talks to get his team prepared before a game or rally them when they were trailing at halftime.

Instead, he was a cerebral man who wanted to outthink and out-prepare his opponents. When it came to motivating his players, he was wont to do that with a single phrase or saying.

These were some of his favorites:

"It's not the will to win, it's the will to prepare."

"Persistence can change failure into extraordinary achievement."

"Football doesn't build character, it reveals it."

If ever Levy wanted to give a longer speech, he was partial to English poetry.

However, he was not going to march into the locker room and upbraid his players, question their manhood, and threaten their jobs. He was a gentleman football coach, an anomaly at a time when most coaches held long and demanding practices, treated their players like property, and paid any price in order for their teams to come away with a win.

Levy struggled throughout a large majority of his coaching career. Prior to being named as the Bills head coach in 1986, Levy had a five-year run in Kansas City from 1978 through 1982, and he had just one winning season before losing his job.

Levy was out of football for a year, but he returned at the professional level with the Chicago Blitz of the United States Football League. The Blitz had been coached previously by George Allen, and when he left to coach in Arizona, he took most of his players with him.

As a result, Levy's team had a 5-13 record, and both the team and the league eventually folded. Levy had worked with general manager Bill Polian in Chicago, and Polian came calling after he became general manager of the Buffalo Bills.

The Bills were stockpiling talent, and when Levy was hired in 1986, they were starting to get better. Levy's first two seasons in Buffalo saw the team improve and get better, but it didn't necessarily show in the record. The Bills were 2-7 after Levy took over in '86 and 7-8 in the strike-altered 1987 season.

But everything came together in 1988, as the Bills went 12-4 and finished first in the AFC East. The Bills defeated the Houston Oilers in their first playoff game before losing in the divisional playoffs to the Cincinnati Bengals, who would eventually make it to the Super Bowl.

The Bills had found their leader in quarterback Jim Kelly, and he had the kind of physical tools that all head coaches were looking for in their leaders. Kelly had the arm strength, quick release, and accuracy to become a great quarterback, but despite the team's record, Levy knew that something wasn't right.

Kelly had a 15-17 touchdown-interception ratio that season, and Levy knew that Kelly was simply much better than that. He was determined to make changes to his offense that would allow Kelly to join the ranks of the top quarterbacks in the game.

The biggest change came the following year when Levy hired mastermind Ted Marchibroda to become the team's offensive coordinator. Marchibroda, another thoughtful coach who rejected the typical football coach's mentality, redesigned the team's offense. He saw the talent the Bills had on offense with Kelly, running back Thurman Thomas, wide receiver Andre Reed, running back Kenneth Davis, and running back Ronnie Harmon, and he decided to up the tempo to put opposing defenses on their heels.

Levy had charged Marchibroda with designing a game plan that would help the Bills to become an offensive juggernaut, and he gave the Bills the "K-Gun" offense. While the Bills would not use this through the entire game, whenever they went to it, it seemed to throw opposing defenses into a state of panic.

"What you want to do as a coach is give your team a chance to be at its best," Levy said. "If it also puts the opponent at a disadvantage, that's a bonus. That's what we did with our K-Gun. I think it brought the best out of Jim, Thurman, and all the rest of our guys, and I don't think our opponents knew what to do. They knew we had options, and they couldn't figure out which option to stop first."

The Bills went 9-7 that season and won the division again, but they came into their own in 1990. They reeled off back-to-back 13-3 seasons in 1990 and '91, and went to the Super Bowl both years. While their record slipped to 11-5 in '92, they also won the AFC title that year and again in '93.

They went to the Super Bowl in four consecutive seasons, and they are the only team in NFL history to manage that feat. Unfortunately for Levy and his players, they lost all four of those Super Bowls.

They almost certainly should have won the first of those appearances when they faced the New York Giants in Super Bowl XXV.

That was the season that the Bills' offense was at its peak, as the Bills scored a league-best 428 points and gave up just 263, which was the sixth-best total in the league.

Kelly had a remarkable season, completing 63.3 percent of his passes for 2,829 yards and compiling a 24-9 touchdown-interception ratio. Thomas rushed for 1,297 yards and also caught 49 passes, while Andre Reed caught 71 passes and was a tremendous runner after the catch. On the defensive side, Bruce Smith had 19.0 sacks while linebacker Darryl Talley had a team-high 123 tackles.

The Bills beat the Dolphins 44-34 in the divisional playoffs, and registered a shocking 51-3 triumph over the Oakland Raiders in the AFC Championship game.

That victory left the Bills as heavy favorites to beat Bill Parcells's New York Giants, who came into the game with backup quarterback Jeff Hostetler under center because starter Phil Simms was injured.

The Giants knew they could not compete with the Bills' firepower, so they took the air out of the ball and tried to maximize each possession by working the clock with their running game.

That strategy served its purpose, as they held a 20-19 lead in the final seconds.

The Bills still had a chance, and if Scott Norwood could have connected on a 47-yard field goal on the Bills' final play, they would have won the game. While Norwood hit the ball squarely, it sailed wide to the right and the Bills were defeated in the game.

They went on to lose two Super Bowls to the Dallas Cowboys and one to the Washington Redskins. None of those games were close.

Obviously, the Super Bowl losses stung Levy and his players, but it didn't keep him from enjoying a Hall of Fame career. Levy would coach the Bills through the 1997 season before retiring from coaching.

The Bills have not been a consistent winner since Levy left, and the team continues to search for a coach who can find a winning formula in Western New York once again.

For the record

Marv Levy
Hall of Fame, 2001
Regular-season record: 143-112-0, .561
Postseason record: 11-8, .579
Four AFC Championships

#16

BUD GRANT

Finally, he said yes.

The year was 1967, and Bud Grant had spent ten years in the Canadian Football League coaching the Winnipeg Blue Bombers. His team had played for six CFL titles and come away with the championship four times.

He knew, and the Minnesota Vikings knew, that he was ready to coach in the NFL. The Vikings had come calling previously. When the franchise had come into existence in 1961, Grant was asked to be the team's initial head coach. However, he knew he had a good thing going in Canada, and if he was good enough to be offered the job when he was thirty-four years old, he reasoned he would be good enough later on.

When the Vikings fired taciturn head coach Norm Van Brocklin in 1966, Grant was ready. The Vikings had the makings of a great team, and he knew he could bring out the best in them.

The first year was a struggle, as the Vikings finished the year with a 3-8-3 record, but after that the Vikings put winning season after winning season on the board. The Vikings went 8-6 in 1968, and made it to the playoffs for the first time when they won their last two games of the year—both on the road to the San Francisco 49ers and the Philadelphia Eagles—to earn a spot in the playoffs.

They were overmatched against the powerful Baltimore Colts, but they played a tough, close game before dropping a 24-14 decision.

That game may have lit the fuse for what followed. The Vikings had a 12-2 team in 1969, led by one of the best defensive lines in the history of the game.

That unit was comprised of Carl Eller, Allen Page, Gary Larsen, and Jim Marshall, and was nicknamed the Purple People Eaters. They played a devastating brand of football, and it was as if that unit took the baton handoff from the Los Angeles Rams' Fearsome Foursome and became the best defensive line in the game.

Offensively, the Vikings were ruffians. Running backs Bill Brown and Dave Osborne handled the bulk of the ground attack, but quarterback Joe Kapp was not afraid to take a hit or dish one out when he had the ball in his hands.

Kapp, another CFL import just like his coach, was not a classic pocket passer. In an era featuring some of the game's finest passers—Johnny Unitas, Sonny Jurgensen, Don Meredith, and John Brodie—Kapp was just as likely to throw a ball that traveled end over end as he was to throw a spiral.

It didn't matter to Grant or the Viking receivers as long as the ball got where it was supposed to go. The Vikings took on the personality of their defense and their quarterback as they rampaged through the NFL that year.

They also took on the image of their coach in Grant, who cut quite a memorable figure with his crew cut and chiseled features. Grant looked like the most serious man in the world and the image painted by the media was that of a tough guy who wanted things done his way ... or else.

But image is not everything. Grant may have looked like he came directly out of central casting to coach a team in the heart of Minnesota's frozen tundra, but he was a thoughtful man who cared about his players as individuals and was more than willing to take part in a practical joke ... or two.

He was serious about football, but he was not the kind of coach who would stay in his office for hours upon hours and demand the same things of his assistants. He wanted to do his job and do it well, and then he wanted to go home and enjoy his family and the great outdoors.

Early in the 1969 season, the Vikings served notice that it would be their year. They pounded the defending NFL champion Baltimore Colts in the second game of the season and that was the first of twelve straight wins. They wouldn't lose again until the regular-season finale against the Atlanta Falcons.

The Vikings were heavy favorites to dominate in the NFL playoffs and go on to represent the league in Super Bowl IV.

That's just what happened. The Vikings struggled before beating the Los Angeles Rams 23-20 in their first playoff game, but overpowered the Cleveland Browns 27-7 in the NFL Championship game. Kapp scored on a seven-yard run early in the game and then threw a seventy-five-yard touchdown pass later in the first quarter to Gene Washington, and the Vikings dominated from that point on.

The Super Bowl turned out to be a disaster. Minnesota was a double-digit favorite over the AFL's Kansas City Chiefs, and they were expected to dominate because of their supposed edge in toughness and skill.

The Chiefs would have none of it, and just like the Jets had done the year before to the Colts, they came into Tulane Stadium and shut down Grant's Vikings by a 23-7 margin.

Losing in the Super Bowl would unfortunately become a theme for the Vikings under Grant. They would make it back to the Super Bowl following the 1973 season, but Don Shula's Miami Dolphins would beat them in the second of their back-to-back championships. The following year, Minnesota would get another shot at the Super Bowl, but they had the misfortune of meeting the Pittsburgh Steelers.

Pittsburgh would become the team of the decade as they won four Super Bowls in the 1970s, and their first victim would be the Vikings.

Grant would get one more chance after the 1976 season, and they would meet another team in the Oakland Raiders that had been frustrated because they had never won a title despite their regular-season excellence in the AFC.

The Vikings, with Fran Tarkenton at quarterback, Chuck Foreman at running back, and wide receivers Ahmad Rashad and Sammy White, were a dynamic offensive team that could score in bunches. They still had the Purple People Eaters up front, and their defense was ferocious.

The Raiders, coached by John Madden and quarterbacked by Ken Stabler, were also loaded. The game had all the elements needed to become a classic.

However, the Raiders were loose and relaxed and played their best game. Grant's Vikings never found their rhythm, and they were badly outplayed. The Raiders pounded them physically and enjoyed a one-sided 32-14 triumph.

Grant's teams were winless in their four Super Bowl chances. While the Vikings fans were heartbroken, Grant was philosophical about the losses.

"You don't look back after any losing game," Grant said. "You look ahead. Life goes on. We never lost a conference championship game and we never lost when the Super Bowl was on the line."

Grant was admired and respected by his players. "Bud was one of the greatest coaches ever in the NFL," Foreman said. "He is a victim of the four losses we had in the Super Bowl, but that doesn't take away from the kind of coach he was. He told players what they needed to hear, not what they wanted to hear. He was fair with everyone, from the superstar to the guy on special teams. He treated every individual like a man."

Grant never brought home the Lombardi Trophy, but his record of consistency is matched by very few coaches. He knew how to get the most out of his players, and he did it without fail.

For the record

Bud Grant
Hall of Fame, 1994
Regular-season record: 158-96-5, .622
Postseason record: 10-12, .455
One NFL Championship, Three NFC Championships

#17

JOE GIBBS

When the Washington Redskins hired Joe Gibbs to be their head coach prior to the 1981 season, it was not a move that had a big impact around the NFL. Gibbs had been an offensive coordinator with the high-powered San Diego Chargers, and while that team was lighting up scoreboards throughout the league, it was difficult to give Gibbs more than a minimal share of the credit.

The Chargers were loaded with talent on the offensive side of the ball with Dan Fouts at quarterback, and receivers like John Jefferson and Kellen Winslow. Gibbs certainly was helping these players, but they were great players on their own. Additionally, head coach Don Coryell had earned a reputation as one of the most thoughtful offensive-minded head coaches in the game, and he deserved quite a bit of credit for San Diego's explosive offense.

But the Redskins knew that Gibbs was smart, organized, and had been successful. They were willing to give him a chance to get their once-glorious franchise going in the right direction.

It was a rough start for Gibbs in the 1981 season, as they dropped their first five games and looked awful in the process. However, Gibbs kept an even keel and did not come close to losing his cool. He was confident that his team would learn the offense he was teaching and would get used to his coaching style.

It didn't take long for that to happen. As inconsistent as they had been in the early part of the season, the Redskins were the most improved team in the league by the end of the season, when they finished 8-8.

Quarterback Joe Theismann learned and adapted to Gibbs's offense, and he proved to be the ideal triggerman to lead the Redskins.

There were no missteps in the 1982 season, although that year the NFL was torn apart by a players strike and the season was shortened to nine games. The Redskins were the best team in the NFC with an 8-1 record, and that earned them the top seed in the NFL's postseason tournament.

They registered convincing postseason victories over the Detroit Lions, Minnesota Vikings, and Dallas Cowboys, and that earned Gibbs's team a spot in the Super Bowl vs. Don Shula's Miami Dolphins.

It could have been a spot for a second-year head coach to feel like he was in over his head, since Shula had already earned a reputation as one of the best coaches in the game's history.

"I suppose I could have been intimidated," Gibbs said. "But I wasn't blocking or tackling Don Shula. I knew I had all the talent I needed on my side and there was no way we wouldn't come up with a great effort against them. I didn't know how it would turn out, but I knew we had the team to compete for 60 minutes."

That's just what the Redskins did, and they came away with a 27-17 victory over the Dolphins in Super Bowl XVII. The Redskins had tremendous balance with Theismann throwing to wide receivers Art Monk and Charlie Brown, and John "Diesel" Riggins running it.

Riggins gave the Redskins the lead in the fourth quarter and took the heart out of the Dolphins with his 43-yard touchdown run.

The Super Bowl would be the first of three Gibbs would win with the Redskins, and he is the only coach to do it with three different quarterbacks. Gibbs's abilities as an offensive innovator made him one of the game's superior minds and it earned him Hall of Fame status in 1996.

Gibbs had developed his offensive philosophies while coaching under Coryell, but he added several of his own innovations.

Gibbs basically invented the position of the H-back position and he also popularized the one-RB set. He wanted to use his bigger, stronger offensive line to get his team's power running game going, and then he wanted to fool opponents with his "trips" and "bunch" formations that made it difficult for opponents to cover Washington's open receivers.

His technical superiority when it came to offensive strategy gave the Redskins a big edge on most opponents, even if the opposition was a more talented team.

Gibbs's goal as a gameplanner was to force the opposition to think about what the Redskins were going to do instead of just playing their game. "Offensively, I wanted to dictate the pace of the game," Gibbs said. "I want to use a fast-paced offense because that makes our team more aggressive and it forces the defense to react to what we were doing."

Gibbs won his other two Super Bowls with Doug Williams and Mark Rypien at quarterback. Each of his three quarterbacks had different strengths, and that speaks to Gibbs's abilities as a head coach.

Theismann was certainly the most accomplished of the three, but Williams had one of the strongest arms of any quarterback to play the game, while Rypien was a mountain of a man who was capable of absorbing big hits from the pass rush and not going down to the ground.

After his third Super Bowl championship following the 1991 season, Gibbs coached one more year before retiring.

After he left the game, Gibbs set up a NASCAR racing team, and he was also successful in that field, as he won three NASCAR cup series championships.

He seemed to be as far away from the NFL as he could possibly be, but Gibbs still maintained an interest in the game as a fan. He thought his coaching days were long over, but new Washington owner Daniel Snyder courted him on a nonstop basis and basically begged him to return to the team.

Gibbs finally relented, and he returned for his second tour of duty with the team in 2004—eight years after he had been named to the Hall of Fame.

The NFL was a much different world in 2004, and Gibbs did not get immediate results, as Washington was a 6-10 team that season. However, Gibbs seemed to have a bit of magic left, as the Redskins improved to 10-6 in 2005, and then made the playoffs.

While they beat Tampa Bay in the wild-card game, they dropped a 20-10 decision when they had to go to Seattle for a divisional playoff game.

The Redskins could not maintain that momentum, as they slipped to 5-11 the following year, which was the worst record of Gibbs's coaching career. They bounced back a bit with a 9-7 record in 2007 that earned them a spot in the postseason, but they got manhandled by the Seahawks once again in the playoffs.

That proved to be the end of Gibbs's career, as he made a final decision to retire.

Throughout his career, Gibbs had proven to be one of the top offensive minds of the game. It can be argued that Gibbs is at the top of the coaching chain when it comes to offensive innovation, and his three Super Bowl titles cement that status.

For the record

> **Joe Gibbs**
> Hall of Fame, 1996
> Regular-season record: 154-94-0, .621
> Postseason record: 17-7, .708
> Three Super Bowl victories

#18

DON CORYELL

Don Coryell wanted to do one thing when he coached in the NFL. He wanted to attack with the passing game and confound opponents with his team's ability to score points in bunches.

Few coaches have ever had the kind of success at installing, developing, and fine-tuning the passing game that Coryell had, first with the St. Louis Cardinals and then the San Diego Chargers.

Today's NFL has largely followed the blueprint that Coryell was responsible for developing in the 1970s. When it came to movement, deception, multiple formations, and vertical pass patterns, Coryell's offense had it all.

"I believe in wide open offense," Coryell said when he was hired by the Cardinals prior to the 1973 season. "I like to throw the ball and I want to attack."

There was never a day in his coaching career that he was not true to his beliefs. He helped transform the unglamorous and ordinary Cardinals into one of the most exciting teams in the league and later turned the Chargers into one of the most explosive teams in NFL history.

Coryell was all about offense, and his attention to defense was not quite what it could have been. That's one of the reasons that his teams would often contend and get to the playoffs, but fail once they got there.

Coryell got a chance to develop his offensive philosophies at the college level first, as the coach at San Diego State. He knew his teams could not compete with national powers like UCLA and USC, so he built a dynamic passing game that often confused opposing defenses.

Coryell also proved adept at developing talented players and coaches. Quarterbacks Brian Sipe and Dennis Shaw came out of his program, as did wide receivers Gary "The Ghost" Garrison, Isaac Curtis, and Haven Moses. He also had top coaches like John Madden and Joe Gibbs on his staff.

When the Cardinals came calling in 1973, he needed a year to get his team turned around and to learn his offense. By 1974, the Cardinals had become one of the most prolific offensive teams in the NFL. Quarterback Jim Hart was a resilient leader and a rubber-armed passer, and he received magnificent protection from an offensive line that included Dan Dierdorf and Conrad "Dirty" Dobler.

They went 10-4 in '74 and followed that with an 11-3 record in '75. They won the NFC East Division title in both years, edging out the Redskins and Cowboys, respectively. Getting the edge on those two powers who were coached by George Allen and Tom Landry, respectively, earned Coryell a tremendous amount of respect among coaches.

However, the Cardinals lost first-round playoff games each year, and that sent Coryell back to the drawing board. He wanted to turn the Cardinals into a true powerhouse, but he rarely got the backing he wanted from the Cardinals' management and ownership.

Coryell grew exasperated when owner Bill Bidwill failed to sign star receiver and returner Terry Metcalf to a fair contract, and that caused Metcalf to abandon the team for the CFL. Coryell's relationship with the team fell apart after that and he left the Cardinals following the '77 season.

He was immediately hired by the Chargers, and they quickly adhered to the principles of Coryell's offense and mastered them. With Dan Fouts at quarterback, the Chargers became the most explosive team in the league. They rolled to a 12-4 record that season, won the AFC West title, and scored 411 points in the process.

However, the Chargers suffered the same playoff failures that Coryell's teams in St. Louis had, as they dropped a 17-14 decision to the Houston Oilers, on their home turf in San Diego.

While criticism started to rain down on Coryell for his playoff failings, Coryell was not daunted and he continued to press forward with his high-powered offense. The 1980 Chargers won the AFC West title again, and this time Coryell finally got his playoff win when the Chargers got the best of the Buffalo Bills in the divisional playoffs.

However, they dropped the AFC Championship game at home to the Oakland Raiders when the visitors played shutdown defense in the second half and held the Chargers to a field goal in the fourth quarter. That enabled the Raiders to win the game and go to the Super Bowl, where they defeated the Philadelphia Eagles.

That was a game that Coryell always felt his team should have been in, because he believed the Chargers were good enough to come away with the title.

The following year, Coryell went a long way to ridding himself of the reputation that he could not win the big game. The Chargers won their third consecutive AFC West title and they scored 478 points in the process. Their offense featured Fouts throwing the ball to Charlie Joiner, Wes Chandler, and tight end Kellen Winslow. They also had two brilliant running backs in Chuck Muncie and James Brooks, and were basically unstoppable with the ball.

The Chargers met the Miami Dolphins at the Orange Bowl in the first round of the playoffs, and this time they were in top form in the postseason.

They jumped out to a 24-0 lead in the first quarter, and they appeared to be running the Dolphins out of their own stadium. But Don Shula's team was nothing if not resilient, and they came back to make it a game by halftime.

The second half was a back-and-forth affair, and the game went into sudden death overtime. While the Dolphins had their chance to come away with the win, Rolf Benirschke's field goal in the extra session allowed the Chargers to win the game and move on to the AFC Championship.

That playoff game is widely recognized as one of the greatest games in NFL history.

The AFC Championship game was another matter. The Chargers were forced to go to frigid Cincinnati to take on the Bengals in the title game. The wind chill reached minus-57 degrees Fahrenheit, and the San Diego offense was frozen solid. The Bengals easily survived and won the game 27-7.

That basically took the heart out of the Chargers. While they made the playoffs again in 1982, that was their last trip to the postseason under Coryell. He continued to coach into the 1986 season before he decided to call it a career.

Coryell's teams never got to the Super Bowl and were just 3-6 in the postseason. But his abilities to come up with an innovative offense made him one of the greatest coaches in the game's history.

Madden, Gibbs, and Fouts have all backed him to become a Hall of Famer. He has reached the semifinals in the voting process from 2011 through 2014, but he has still not been admitted to the Canton shrine.

"It's just wrong that Don isn't in the Hall of Fame," Madden said. "There are some things that just don't make sense, and this is one of them."

For the record

Don Coryell
Regular-season record: 111-83-1, .572
Postseason record: 3-6, .333
Five division championships

#19

WEEB EWBANK

Weeb Ewbank didn't look like a tough football coach, and he was not known for making demands of his players and asking them to do everything he told them to do.

Even though he coached in an era when football coaches were often tyrants who could not be questioned by their players or assistants, Ewbank was more of the thinking man's coach who brought out the best in his players and helped them achieve great things.

Ewbank led two teams to perhaps the most symbolic and important victories in the NFL. He led the Baltimore Colts to the 1958 NFL Championship in a game that has often been described as the greatest game in NFL history.

The Colts had a marvelous team in 1958 that featured Johnny Unitas at quarterback, Alan Ameche running the ball, Raymond Berry at wide receiver, and a destructive defense. The Colts finished 9-3 that season and won the West Division by a game over the Chicago Bears and Los Angeles Rams, who both finished 8-4.

They earned a spot in the NFL Championship game against the New York Giants, who had finished in a tie with the Cleveland Browns for first in the East Division. The Giants had emerged victorious in a playoff game to decide the title, and they hosted the Colts at Yankee Stadium in the title game.

It was a back-and-forth bruising affair, and the Giants appeared to be on their way to victory when Frank Gifford scored a fourth-quarter touchdown after taking a fifteen-yard pass from Charlie Conerly.

However, the Colts tied it on a late field goal by Steve Myhra, and the NFL had the first overtime game in its history.

Unitas led the Colts on a historic march in the extra session, and they pounded the ball down the field. Finally, he stuck the ball in Ameche's belly, and the big fullback pounded into the end zone from a yard out and the Colts earned the championship.

That game, more than any one single event, is considered to be the game that turned professional football into America's national sport. The game captured the nation's attention, and it translated so well to the audience viewing the game on television that it triggered a love affair between a nation's sports fans and the sport.

Ewbank would lead the Colts to the NFL championship again the following year, and they would remain a competitive team after that, but they were supplanted by the Green Bay Packers as the best team in the West.

The Colts fired Ewbank after the team went 7-7 in 1962, and the decision angered Ewbank. He felt like he was being blamed even though he had led the Colts to two titles and the team was capable of bouncing back and competing again. He had also helped develop Unitas into perhaps the game's best quarterback.

But Ewbank was not out of work for very long. The American Football League started play in 1960, and that meant that there were eight more opportunities for head coaches to gain employment. The worst of those teams may have been the New York Titans, who went bankrupt after the 1962 season.

However, the team did not stay insolvent very long, and it was rescued by businessman Sonny Werblin, who renamed the team as the Jets, and the first big move that he made was to hire Ewbank as his head coach.

Shortly after hiring Ewbank, the Jets drafted Alabama quarterback Joe Namath, and Werblin was able to convince the star to sign with his team over the NFL's St. Louis Cardinals. Something about the Broadway lights appealed to Namath, and he got an even bigger boost as he gained the opportunity to work with Ewbank.

Namath was one of the most gifted passers to ever play the game. He had a rocket for an arm and one of the quickest releases that pro football observers had ever seen. Namath could throw the ball forty yards with a flick of his wrist, and the sound of the ball whizzing through the air was unlike the sound of any other quarterback in the game.

But Namath was far from a finished product. He was a raw talent with an ego. Ewbank had to convince him that he had a lot to learn about winning at the professional level and that he could give him the knowledge he needed to read defenses, call the correct plays, and help make his team a winner.

It was not an easy relationship, but Namath ultimately came around to embrace his teacher and absorb his lessons. The two would form one of the greatest coach-quarterback partnerships, as Namath would blossom into one of the best quarterbacks in the AFL.

The Jets had a brilliant 1968 season and won the AFL's East Division with an 11-3 record. They were expected to fall short in the AFL Championship game against the relentless Oakland Raiders, but the Jets hung tough on their home turf at Shea Stadium and managed a 27-23 victory when Namath hit wide receiver Don Maynard with the winning touchdown pass late in the fourth quarter.

That set the scene for Super Bowl III, in which the Jets were expected to be cannon fodder for the powerful Baltimore Colts.

The same team that fired Ewbank six years earlier was clearly the best team in the NFL that year, and the Jets didn't appear to have a chance.

The Colts were bigger, faster, and stronger physically, and appeared to have an edge at every position with the possible exception of quarterback, where Earl Morrall had taken over for the injured Unitas.

The oddsmakers installed the Colts as 18-point favorites, and nearly every prominent sportswriter of the day thought the Colts would win easily.

However, Ewbank had a bunch of true believers in the Jets' locker room, and they shocked the Colts 16-7. Namath did not have a huge statistical day, but he picked apart the Baltimore defense with short passes, and the Jets' running game with Matt Snell and Emerson Boozer confounded Baltimore.

Colts coach Don Shula was perplexed by the Jets, and his offense could never figure out the Jets' defense.

Ewbank described the victory in Super Bowl III as the most satisfying moment of his career. The Jets' victory was not only a win for the team, but also it was a major triumph for the AFL.

The NFL had regularly looked down its nose and pooh-poohed the younger league, and those associated with the older league did not think any AFL squad could compete with its top teams.

The Jets' win allowed the league to celebrate and feel good about itself. "I remember how happy I was when the Jets won that game," said Kansas City Chiefs quarterback Len Dawson. "We would win the Super Bowl the next year, but the Jets' win did so much for all of us. I had tears in my eyes. Weeb Ewbank just did some great job of preparing his team and coaching it."

Ewbank couldn't have been more satisfied. "I gave the AFL a win in the Super Bowl, and it was over Baltimore," Ewbank said. "That was certainly a moment to savor."

Ewbank's legacy was sealed when he led the Colts to consecutive NFL championships, but he became one of the game's greatest coaches when he steered the Jets to the greatest upset in the history of professional football.

For the record

Weeb Ewbank
Hall of Fame, 1978
Regular-season record: 130–129–7, .621
Postseason record: 4–1, .800
One Super Bowl victory
Two NFL championships

#20

MIKE HOLMGREN

When Mike Holmgren was named head coach of the Green Bay Packers in 1992, general manager Ron Wolf had every confidence that he had made the right choice to bring the organization back to the glory that it had not known since Vince Lombardi was at the helm in the 1960s.

Holmgren had been Bill Walsh's right-hand man in San Francisco for years, and he was the one with whom Walsh would discuss his offensive theories. It was not simply a case of Walsh teaching Holmgren; he was the beneficiary of Holmgren's knowledge and philosophy of offensive football as well.

Additionally, Holmgren had the kind of personality that allowed him to relate well to his players and reach them with a dynamism that Walsh never had. That's what Wolf had recognized, and that's why he knew that Holmgren would be successful.

"He fills a room with that presence that you just can't measure," Wolf said. "He has that Bill Walsh type of confidence where he just knows what he does is right."

It was clear that Holmgren knew the game like few others, and that knowledge was put to the test in 1992. Not only was that his first year as head coach with the Packers, but it was also the year that Wolf acquired a quarterback named Brett Favre.

Favre had been highly thought of when the Atlanta Falcons drafted him in the second round of the 1991 draft. However, head coach Jerry Glanville was not overly impressed with the strong-armed quarterback from the University of Southern Mississippi, and when the Packers inquired about trading for him, Glanville had no objections.

Holmgren and Favre would become tied at the hip shortly after he came to Green Bay. In his first training camp with the Packers, Holmgren saw the same thing that Glanville had seen in Atlanta—a raw prospect with overwhelming physical skills, but also a player who was largely undisciplined and mistake-prone.

Favre seemed confused by nearly all of the assignments he had in practice and the preseason, and he did not figure in the Packers' immediate plans as the '92 season began.

The Packers had Don Majkowski as their starting quarterback, who was known as "The Magic Man" for his ability to escape pressure when all seemed lost and then make a big play. That was overstating his abilities just a bit, but the ever-hopeful Green Bay fans had little to work with.

That would soon change, as Holmgren was forced to tap Favre on the shoulder when Majkowski got hurt in the third game of the season against the Cincinnati Bengals. Favre threw a fourth-quarter touchdown pass to Sterling Sharpe and then he got the ball back with his team trailing 23-17 in the waning moments. He fired a game-winning, 35-yard touchdown pass to Kitrick Taylor in the game's final moments, and Holmgren knew he had his quarterback.

Holmgren looked at Favre the way Michelangelo looked at the ceiling of the Sistine Chapel. He knew there was an overwhelming amount of work to be done, but he also knew he had the finest raw material he could ever hope to work with.

Holmgren was an offensive master who had earned the respect of Walsh, and now he had a quarterback with overwhelming arm strength, a quick release, and brilliant talent. That they came together in the NFL's smallest outpost in Green Bay didn't matter a bit.

The Packers had been one of the NFL's most frequent losers prior to the 1992 season, having endured twenty-one losing seasons in twenty-five years since Vince Lombardi had left the team after Super Bowl II. But the combination of Holmgren, Wolf, and Favre gave long-suffering Packers fans hope that a major change was at hand.

The Packers would finish with a 9-7 record in '92, and when Wolf pulled off a major coup and signed future Hall of Fame defensive end Reggie White as a free agent in '93, the Packers became legitimate contenders in the NFL.

Holmgren knew how to get the most out of his players. His first priority was to continue to work with Favre so that his raw talent could be turned into skill and ability. It was not an easy assignment, as Favre often made mistakes in practice that left observers and teammates smacking their foreheads in frustration.

Holmgren proved to be a knowledgeable, competent, and successful teacher. Favre would go on to hone his skills and turn into one of the greatest quarterbacks the game has ever known. The key for Holmgren was not just limiting Favre's mistakes. It was keeping his competitive and creative spirit alive.

Holmgren was also a skilled game planner who could look at an opponent on film, find their weaknesses, and then provide an attack plan that regularly resulted in victory. He also knew how to relate to his players with his fully developed personality.

He could laugh with them, joke with them, excoriate them, and make demands. He showed all sides of his personality to his players, and they responded well to him.

Holmgren's Packers made the playoffs in '93, as they beat Detroit in the wild-card game before losing to Jimmy Johnson's Dallas Cowboys. Favre was instrumental in both of those outcomes, as his remarkable forty-yard touchdown pass to Sharpe gave the Packers the winning points in the fourth quarter against the Lions, and his two interceptions played a key role in the loss to Green Bay.

The Cowboys would eliminate the Packers from the postseason following the '94 and '95 seasons as well, and there was a feeling that Favre's spectacular arm would continue to wow fans and impress the media, but that his mistakes would always find a way to be costly to the team.

Holmgren and Favre knew of that reputation, and they stepped up their game in the 1996 season. They rolled to a 13-3 regular season, and most of their wins were of the dominant variety. They humbled the San Francisco 49ers in the divisional playoffs and Carolina Panthers in the NFC Championship game, and that earned them a trip to the Super Bowl for the first time in twenty-nine years.

The Packers went to Super Bowl XXXI in New Orleans against the upstart New England Patriots, and it was a dream game for the Packers. Favre threw two touchdown passes and did not have an interception, White had three sacks, and explosive Desmond Howard had a ninety-nine-yard kickoff return for a touchdown.

The Packers won the game and brought the Vince Lombardi Trophy back home to Green Bay. Holmgren, Favre, and White were heroes in Wisconsin.

The Packers may have been an even better team the following year, and they went back to the Super Bowl following another 13-3 season. They were expected to beat a Denver Broncos team that was trying to break the AFC's twelve-game losing streak in the Super Bowl.

However, the Packers came up short in the game and dropped a 31-24 decision that shocked the football world.

Holmgren would coach one more season with the Packers before he decided to leave the team. Instead of merely coaching an NFL team, Holmgren had a great desire to be responsible for personnel procurement. He wanted to bring in his own players as well as coach the team.

He found that opportunity in Seattle. The Seahawks gave him the chance to build a team and coach it, and after an up-and-down six years, he turned the Seahawks into a Super Bowl team in 2005. While they dropped a brutally tough 21-10 decision to the Pittsburgh Steelers, Holmgren accomplished what he had set off to do when he left Green Bay.

Holmgren coached through the 2008 season, and his final season was a 4-12 disappointment. While his coaching career appears to have ended with a whimper, he put together a remarkable career that featured the rejuvenation of one of the NFL's flagship franchises and the development of one of the game's best quarterbacks.

For the record

Mike Holmgren
Regular-season record: 161-111-0, .592
Postseason record: 13-11, .542
One Super Bowl victory

#21

BUM PHILLIPS

Homespun and folksy from the top of his head to the tips of his toes, Bum Phillips had the opportunity to coach the Houston Oilers in the mid-1970s. At the time, the Oilers were a laughable team competing in the same division with the Pittsburgh Steelers, who may have put together the greatest team in the history of the game.

Phillips may have seemed like a laughable bumpkin, but he was one of the greatest coaches the game has ever known. He combined a personable manner with his superior instincts for football and he turned the Oilers into a spectacular team.

While they were never able to overcome Chuck Noll's Steelers, they carved out a niche and developed a loyal following that has rarely been reached.

Philips and the "Luv Ya Blue" Oilers became a national team in a 1978 Monday Night Football game against the Miami Dolphins. In that game, the Oilers rode a magical performance from Hall of Fame running back Earl Campbell to a 35-30 victory.

Campbell carried 28 times for 199 yards and four touchdowns, including an eighty-one-yard run down the sidelines that is one of the greatest plays in the history of the Monday night series.

Phillips had started his NFL career as the defensive coordinator for Sid Gillman's San Diego Chargers from 1967 through 1970. When Gillman became both general manager and head coach of the Houston Oilers several years later, he brought Phillips with him, and Phillips was the defensive coordinator for the Oilers in 1974.

Gillman left the Oilers in a dispute with owner Bud Adams after that season, and the owner then turned to Phillips to become his head coach. Phillips was a defensive specialist, but he used his time with Gillman well and learned the principles of developing a high-powered offense quite well.

The Oilers could throw the ball and attack with the big play. He was not hesitant to let quarterback Dan Pastorini cut loose and wing the ball, and his quarterback had one of the top wide receivers in the game in Ken "Double-0" Burrough catching passes.

The Oilers were an up-and-down team from 1975 through 1977, but when they added Campbell in 1978, it changed their personality, talent level, and made the rest of the league take notice.

"I became a much better coach once we drafted Earl Campbell," Phillips said. "One of the things I learned throughout my coaching days was that the more good players I had, the better a coach I became. That's pretty much the way it goes in this business.

You show me a good coach and I'll show you a coach with good players."

That obviously made sense, but Phillips was always quite modest about his own abilities and never liked taking credit for anything his players did.

However, he was quick to pay compliments to other coaches. His assessment of Hall of Famer Don Shula during the 1970s has stood the test of time and is one of the most memorable quotes in the history of the game.

"He could take his'n and beat your'n," Phillips said, "and then he could take your'n and beat his'n."

The line, delivered in his thick Texas drawl, may have been amusing to those outside of Texas because of his quaint delivery, but football people appreciated his ability to get to the heart of the matter quickly.

In an era when coaches held all the power and were often quick to use it by criticizing and castigating players in front of teammates or with the media, Phillips was never one to follow that game plan.

He hated confrontations with his players and he refused to get in their face or take complaints to the public. If he had a problem with the way an individual player was performing, he simply changed players. He did not get into a war of words or have feuds with his athletes.

He wanted everybody on the same page, and he was able to get his Oilers to play at a very consistent level. The Oilers may have been the second-best team in the league in the 1978 and '79 seasons, but the Pittsburgh Steelers were the best team in the league.

The Oilers were forced to go to Pittsburgh after both of those seasons to play Chuck Noll's Steelers in the AFC title games, and they couldn't beat them in either one.

Pittsburgh's defense was brutal throughout their championship run during the 1970s, but the 1978 and '79 teams were much better offensively than the two championship teams earlier in the decade.

The Oilers were very talented on both sides of the ball, but they just couldn't match up with the Steelers, no matter what Phillips did to get his team prepared. The Oilers were humbled in the 1978 AFC Title game by a 34-5 margin, and they played a bit better the following year before losing 27-13 in that title game.

He tried to get his team fired up for the '80 season by telling a crowd of supportive Houstonians in the Astrodome that the team was capable of doing better. "Last year, we knocked on the door," he said. "This year, we beat on it. Next year, we are going to kick the son of a bitch in."

The crowd roared its approval, but the Oilers were never able to live up to Phillips's promise. The team suffered some attrition, and Phillips developed problems with Houston general manager Ladd Herzeg.

Those difficulties ultimately led to Phillips's dismissal from the team, and it can be argued that the Oilers never recovered from the loss of their beloved head coach.

Phillips's players were enraged when he was dismissed. All-Pro linebacker Robert Brazile launched into a staunch defense of his coach, saying some players should have been cut and so should some of the team's management, but not Phillips.

"It's a joke," Brazile snorted. "For everything he's done for this team. He was a father to most players, not just a coach. He treated us like men."

Philips would go on to coach the New Orleans Saints for five seasons, but the best he could ever do in New Orleans was an 8-8 season in 1983.

His head coaching career came to an end following the 1985 season, but his son Wade became a respected defensive coordinator and a fine head coach himself.

The Phillips years were among the best in Houston Oilers history, and his ability to get the most from his players remains his legacy and best characteristic.

For the record

Bum Phillips
Regular-season record: 82-77-0, .516
Postseason record: 4-3, .571

#22

MARTY SCHOTTENHEIMER

The numbers explain that Marty Schottenheimer was one of the great coaches in the history of the game. He won 200 games as an NFL head coach, a figure that ranks him seventh on the all-time list. He's just behind names like Bill Belichick and Paul Brown, and just ahead of Chuck Noll and Dan Reeves.

But for all of Schottenheimer's success, his postseason struggles tormented him and underscored what may have been the weaknesses in Schottenheimer's coaching style.

Schottenheimer coached four teams during his coaching career that lasted from 1984 through 2006. He led the Browns, Chiefs, and Chargers to a series of successful campaigns, and he had one season in Washington that was rather forgettable, as his straight-forward and demanding style didn't fit in with owner Daniel Snyder.

But going back to the beginning, Schottenheimer had a way about him that was always different from the mainstream, and he embraced those differences. He didn't try to go along with the latest trends or even know what they were. He was his own man and he didn't try to impress his peers, his players, the fans, or the owners.

He wanted to win and he did it his way. He liked to play a conservative brand of football that features a strong running attack, taking the ball away from his opponents and being sound in the kicking game.

These decidedly unsexy features may be the reason he had a 5-13 postseason record, but they are also the reasons his teams went 200-126-1 during the regular season.

When it comes down to it, his first playoff team in Cleveland was almost certainly the closest he ever came to taking one of his teams to the Super Bowl.

In the 1986 season, Schottenheimer was in his third season at the helm of the Browns. He had Bernie Kosar at quarterback, a pair of hard-nosed running backs in Kevin Mack and Earnest Byner, and one of the hardest-hitting and nastiest defenses in the NFL.

The Browns were a relentless team that knew how to put away an opponent when they got them down. While they did not have explosive superstars, they were a sharp bunch that took advantage of mistakes by their opponents. They won the AFC Central Division with a 12-4 record, and that mark also gave them home field advantage throughout the playoffs.

They were nearly upset in the opening round by the New York Jets, as they found themselves down by 10 points in the fourth quarter. However, a one-yard touchdown run by Mack and a field goal by Mark Moseley—the last of the NFL's straight-ahead kickers—sent the game into overtime.

The Jets and Browns slugged back-and-forth and accomplished nothing until Moseley booted a 27-yard field goal early in the second overtime to put the Browns in the AFC title game.

Cleveland's Municipal Stadium was a rabid Dawg Pound when the Denver Broncos came calling in January of 1987, and the Browns were much better than they had been the previous week against the Jets.

However, even though Kosar hit wide receiver Brian Brennan with a forty-eight-yard touchdown pass late in the fourth quarter to give the Browns a 20-13 lead, Schottenheimer knew his team was in anything but a safe position.

The Broncos had John Elway, and he was rapidly becoming one of the greatest quarterbacks in the game. He would make occasional errant throws and poor decisions, but he had the strongest arm in the game, brilliant athleticism, and a penchant for coming through when his team needed him most.

When the Broncos botched the ensuing kickoff and started the possession at their own two-yard line, it looked like the Browns were going to be making a trip to their first Super Bowl.

However, Elway was undaunted. He negotiated his team up the field, using his legs to escape the pass rush and firing hard strikes to his receivers.

The Cleveland crowd had been bawdy when Elway started the drive, but they grew quieter and quieter as Elway led his team upfield in the final moments.

Schottenheimer had no way of slowing Elway down, and the quarterback culminated the drive in the final seconds when he hit wide receiver Mark Jackson with a perfectly thrown five-yard touchdown pass that hit the receiver in the chest as he was going low to make the catch.

The air went out of the huge stadium after that play. Even though it only tied the score, everyone seemed to know what would happen in overtime.

It did. The Broncos moved the ball smartly down the field, and their barefoot kicker Rich Karlis drilled a thirty-three-yard field goal to send the Broncos to Super Bowl XXI and left the Browns and their fans to cry in their beer.

A year later, the two teams met in Denver for the AFC title, and the Broncos rolled to an early 21–0 lead that was still 28–10 in the third quarter. That's when the Browns mounted a huge comeback behind Byner's running prowess and Kosar's passing acumen.

Late in the fourth quarter, the Browns started a drive from their own two-yard line to tie the game, just as Denver had done the year before. However, this time the dream died in heartbreak.

Kosar stuck the ball in Byner's midsection and the Cleveland line gave him the hole he needed. Byner broke into the open and just as he was preparing to take the stride that would let him into the end zone, Denver defensive back Jeremiah Castille stripped the ball from him and the Broncos recovered the ball.

Schottenheimer coached one more season in Cleveland before moving on to Kansas City. He had nine winning years out of ten with the Chiefs, and his 1997 team won thirteen games. However, Schottenheimer's Kansas City teams were just 3–7 in the postseason.

It was more of the same in San Diego, as he had a 12–4 team in 2004 and a 14–2 team in his final season in 2006. However, the Marty Ball philosophy failed in the playoffs in both years.

Schottenheimer never altered his ways, and his stubbornness cost him in the end. He was clearly a brilliant regular-season coach, but his intractability cost him in the postseason.

It will probably prevent one of the most driven and organized coaches from ending up in the Hall of Fame.

For the record

Marty Schottenheimer
Regular-season record: 200–126–1, .613
Postseason record: 5–13, .278
Eight division championships

#23

HANK STRAM

There is a plethora of diva wide receivers, and quite a few who man the quarterback position.

But when it came to the diva as head coach, Hank Stram may be at the top of the list.

Stram was always perfectly tailored and looking sharp when he took the sidelines for the Kansas City Chiefs (or for the Dallas Texans or New Orleans Saints), and he always demanded that his players and assistant coaches looked good as well.

There was nothing casual about the Stram style, as he paraded the sidelines like a proud rooster.

But there was a lot more to Stram than making a statement with his looks and his clothes. He was one of the most innovative coaches of his time, and he was also exceptional when it came to player development.

Stram began his head coaching career when the American Football League came into existence in the 1960 season. League founder Lamar Hunt hired Stram to coach his Dallas Texans, and his team was a contender right from the start and won its first AFL title in 1963.

While the Texans were a strong team on the field, Hunt's AFL entry was not going to be able to compete long-term with the Cowboys on a financial basis, so he moved his team to Kansas City, where they became the Chiefs.

Stram had assembled a team of strong players that included Len Dawson at quarterback, Mike Garrett at running back, and Otis Taylor at wide receiver. The defense may have been even better, with stars like defensive end Buck Buchanan, middle linebacker Willie Lanier, outside linebacker Bobby Bell, and safety Johnny Robinson.

Stram was not content merely to play with the standard formations of the day. His offense would shift regularly to confuse opposing defenses and he would regularly use a 3-4 formation so his sensational group of linebackers could use their athletic ability to dominate games.

Stram liked to use two tight end formations long before they became popular in the NFL, and he would "stack" his defensive players so they could play without being bogged down by blockers. Instead of positioning his linebacker in the gaps between his defensive linemen, he would often place the linebackers directly behind a defensive tackle or end so they could play with freedom.

Stram explained his theories regularly to the media, and I interviewed him on several occasions. "With a player like Bobby Bell, why would I want to make him take on a blocker before he went after the ball carrier?" Stram asked rhetorically. "He was so fast and such a good athlete, I wanted him to take a direct line into the backfield or to the ball carrier. There was no reason to ask him to take on a blocker first if he didn't have to."

When Stram explained something, you always got the feeling that he believed anyone who didn't see it his way was lacking in intelligence.

Stram and his Chiefs won the AFL championship in 1966, when they beat the Buffalo Bills. That victory earned the Chiefs a spot in the first Super Bowl, a game that was known as the "AFL-NFL Championship Game" at the time.

The Chiefs played Vince Lombardi's vaunted Green Bay Packers, and none of the experts or oddsmakers figured the Chiefs would be anything more than cannon fodder in the game.

The final score was 35-10 in favor of the Packers, and it seemed like Green Bay was the dominant team from the end result. Though that may have been true in the second half, in the first half, the Chiefs played the Packers on nearly even terms and trailed by just a 14-10 margin.

Kansas City made mistakes in the second half, and the Packers took advantage of them to build a significant margin.

Lombardi damned the Chiefs with faint praise after the game. "Kansas City has a fine ball club," Lombardi told the media after the game. "But I think there are four or five teams in the National Football League that are better than they are. There, I said it."

Lombardi's remarks chafed Stram throughout the offseason. The AFL and NFL teams played exhibition games against each other for the first time in 1967, and when the Chiefs met George Halas and the Chicago Bears in the preseason, he decided to take on Lombardi's insult as a challenge.

The Chiefs beat the Bears up and down the field throughout the exhibition game, which they played as if it were a playoff game. The Chiefs ripped the Bears 66-14, and there was no let-up at any point in the game.

"This was no ordinary exhibition game," said former Chicago Bears linebacker, the late Doug Buffone. "They were out to make a point from the start, and they made it. We were there to play a preseason game, and they wanted to mop the field with us."

Stram and his Chiefs were an excellent team in 1967, but they were not quite as good as the Oakland Raiders, who won the AFL championship that year and also lost to the Packers in the Super Bowl. The following year, the Chiefs lost a playoff game to the Raiders after both teams finished with 12-2 records.

Despite seemingly superior personnel, the Raiders could not get past Joe Namath and the New York Jets in the AFL title game.

The Jets would go on to beat the Raiders in the AFL title game and then register perhaps the biggest upset in pro football history when they defeated the Baltimore Colts 16-7 in Super Bowl III.

It was a victory celebrated by every AFL member, including Stram. "I remember there was just this feeling of great pride when New York won the game," Stram said. "I knew we were doing something special in the AFL and there was not a doubt in my mind about that. But when I had a chance to see the Jets prove it on the field against their super team, it was wonderful.

"Of course, we wanted to go out there and do it ourselves."

Stram didn't have to wait long. The Chiefs beat the Jets in the playoffs and then defeated the Raiders in the final AFL Championship game before that league merged with the NFL.

That gave the Chiefs a chance to go back to the Super Bowl against the supposedly superior Minnesota Vikings. Minnesota was a huge double-digit favorite, and the Purple People Eaters were supposed to punish the AFL representatives for the humiliation the NFL had been handed the year before when the Jets beat the Colts.

If anything, the Chiefs were more dominant than the Jets had been, as they rolled past the Vikings 23-7 in Super Bowl IV.

That Super Bowl became one of the most famous games in NFL history, and helped make NFL Films a huge success. Stram agreed to wear a tiny microphone on his finely tailored suit, and everything he said during the game was captured for posterity.

The gregarious Stram was at his most colorful as his team played with poise and momentum. He urged Dawson and the offense to keep "matriculating the ball down the field" and when running back Mike Garrett scored a first-half touchdown on a running play, Stram played to the cameras by repeating the play call "64 toss-power trap" repeatedly.

Stram loved to strut and preen, but he had the substance to go with his style. His teams won three AFL championships and one Super Bowl, and he was among the most innovative coaches of his time.

Additionally, he helped open doors for African-American players that had been closed and he was always appreciated and loved by his players.

Bell said that Stram would often exasperate his players with his demanding ways in practice, but his players always thought of him with warmth and fondness. "We knew he cared about us," Bell said. "That was the bottom line. He cared about us as people, and that's why we always played for him."

Stram appreciated his players and he gave them inventive and innovative game plans. He built championship teams and helped write some of the most important chapters in the history of professional football.

For the record

> **Hank Stram**
> Hall of Fame, 2003
> Regular-season record: 131-97-10, .575
> Postseason record: 5-3, .625
> One Super Bowl victory
> Two AFL Championships

#24

CHUCK KNOX

By the time Chuck Knox got his first opportunity to become a head coach in the NFL, he had become an expert in what it took to be successful.

Knox had spent the start of his pro football career as the offensive line coach for the New York Jets under Weeb Ewbank, and the main part of his job was making sure that the line gave quarterback Joe Namath protection.

After he left the Jets and moved on to the Detroit Lions, it was more of the same thing. He needed to find a way to protect Lions quarterback Bill Munson, who had a strong arm but lacked mobility.

During a five-year run in Detroit under head coach Joe Schmidt, Knox picked up on what it took to put pressure on an opposing quarterback. Since it was his job to make sure his quarterback was protected and upright, he spent most of his time figuring out how to attack the pocket and then coming up with the game plan that would defeat the strategy.

By the time the Los Angeles Rams came calling so he could become their head coach in 1973, the forty-one-year-old Knox knew as much about attacking the pocket and protecting the quarterback as any coach in the NFL did.

He had immediate success with the Rams. His team went 12-2 in his first season, and they did it with flair. The Rams scored 388 points that season with John Hadl at quarterback, Lawrence McCutcheon running the ball, and Harold Jackson making big plays through the air.

The defense was just as accomplished, and a unit that featured Fred Dryer, Jack "Hacksaw" Reynolds, and Isiah Robertson gave up just 178 points. The plus–210-point differential was by far the best in the league, and the Rams went into the postseason as the odds–on favorite to represent the NFC in the Super Bowl.

But despite all the team's regular-season success, there was something wrong in the playoffs. The Rams lost 27-16 to the Dallas Cowboys. Dallas jumped to a quick 17-0 lead, and the Rams were never able to get back in the game.

Unfortunately for Knox, that first season would become a pattern that he and his teams would repeat regularly throughout the twenty-two years he coached in the NFL. The hard-nosed Knox would often get the most out of his team by building a powerful running attack, limiting turnovers, and creating pressure with its defense.

However, when the Rams continued to stick with their conservative strategy once they got into the postseason, they were relatively easy to figure out for top coaches like Tom Landry of the Dallas

Cowboys and Bud Grant of the Minnesota Vikings. If a team was going to load the box and go all out to stop the Rams' power running game, Los Angeles was going to be at a disadvantage.

Knox coached the Rams for five years, and while they made the playoffs every year, they never got out of the NFC Championship and made it to the Super Bowl.

Perhaps their best chance to make that happen came in the 1975 season when the Rams rolled to another 12-2 mark and easily dispatched Don Coryell's St. Louis Cardinals in the divisional round of the playoffs.

However, even though they were heavy favorites against the wild-card-winning Dallas Cowboys in the NFC Championship game, they got embarrassed badly by a 37-7 score. Even though the Rams were bigger, stronger, younger, and faster than the Cowboys, they got outplayed and outsmarted at every turn.

After five years of scintillating regular-season success and post-season disappointment, Knox and Rams owner Carroll Rosenbloom mutually decided to part company. Knox went to the struggling Buffalo Bills, and he turned that team around in his third year.

The Bills had back-to-back playoff seasons in 1980 and 1981. While they dropped a playoff game to San Diego in '80, they came back with a fire the following year.

Quarterback Joe Ferguson and running back Joe Cribbs gave them a formidable offense, and the Bills scored a thrilling 31-27 victory over the Jets in the wild-card round before losing in Cincinnati the following week.

Knox would leave the Bills after the strike-torn 1982 season and return to the West Coast. He headed the Seattle Seahawks operation, and he was bound and determined to take an undisciplined team and turn them into champions.

His first season in Seattle was a magical one. The Seahawks were a .500 team through fourteen weeks, and they needed to win their last two games to make the playoffs. They beat the New York Giants on the road and then hammered the New England Patriots 24-6 in the season finale to earn a playoff spot with a 9-7 record.

They met the Denver Broncos in the wild-card game, and Knox's Seahawks overpowered Denver 31-7. Considering the quarterback matchup of John Elway vs. Dave Krieg, most found the Seahawks' victory shocking.

Expectations continued to be low for the Seahawks, who were expected to be cannon fodder for Miami and Dan Marino in the next round. There was no reason to expect the Seahawks to stay close to the explosive Dolphins, but Krieg was sharp in his passing and running back Curt Warner (113 yards and two touchdowns) showed why he was one of the top running backs in the league. The Seahawks left Miami with a 27-20 victory.

The Seahawks met the Los Angeles Raiders in the AFC Championship game, and they had beaten the Raiders twice in the regular season. However, the Raiders were too deep and too strong and ultimately prevailed in a 30-14 decision.

Knox and the Seahawks were determined not to fall short in the following season. They rolled to a 33-0 victory over the Cleveland Browns in the season opener, but the Seattle locker room was like a morgue after the game.

Warner, perhaps the best running back in the game, tore up his knee and was lost for the season. Assistant coach Joe Vitt explained how Knox refused to let his team feel sorry for itself.

"Everybody's looking to Chuck for reassurance, and I'll never forget what he did," Vitt told the *Los Angeles Times*. "He comes out, gets the team together and says, 'Now we're going to find out who the believers are.'

"He says, 'Nobody is going to believe in this talent. There are teams around the league right now saying the Seahawks are finished. There are coaches and players right here who don't believe we're going to win. Now we're going to find out who the believers are.'

"Then he went out to practice and he was right in the huddle, running the plays, and he wouldn't let anyone feel sorry for themselves. I remember him challenging the defense. He had stepped up to another level, intensity-wise, and everybody out there realized he was in this thing to win. They joined him."

The Seahawks went on to win the AFC West that year with a 12-4 record. They found a way to beat the Raiders in the postseason, but they lost their chance to advance to the AFC Championship when the Dolphins ripped them 31-10.

But the 1984 season was vintage Chuck Knox. His team had suffered an injury that would have cut the heart out of most teams, and all the Seahawks did was play their best football.

Knox would coach the Seahawks through the 1991 season, and then return to the Rams for three more seasons before calling it a career after the 1994 season.

Knox never changed his approach, and while his hard work and run-first style never won a championship, it earned him 186 regular season wins, a figure that ranks tenth in NFL history.

For the record

> **Chuck Knox**
> Regular-season record: 186-147-1, .559
> Postseason record: 7-11, .389
> Seven division championships

#25

BILL COWHER

The hard-nosed, jut-jawed head coach of the Pittsburgh Steelers didn't appear to have much of a chance to make a name for himself in the NFL.

He was a linebacker out of North Carolina State, and he wasn't even drafted in 1979. He was invited to try out for the Philadelphia Eagles that year, and made it all the way to the final cut when head coach Dick Vermeil let him go.

Despite that rejection, he earned a spot with the Cleveland Browns and he eventually became captain of their special teams. The Eagles, who had cut him three years earlier, traded a ninth-round draft choice to reacquire him to lift their special teams play.

A knee injury ended his playing career in 1984, but he had demonstrated maximum effort every minute that he had worn an NFL uniform, and that impressed Marty Schottenheimer. He hired Cowher as an assistant coach in Cleveland, and Schottenheimer took the enthusiastic Cowher to Kansas City when the Chiefs hired him.

The apprenticeship served Cowher well, as he learned quite a bit about coaching from Schottenheimer, who was regularly viewed as one of the most prepared men in the NFL.

Cowher had the desire to be a head coach, and when Chuck Noll decided to call it a career after the 1991 season, Cowher wanted the position.

Cowher was decidedly old-school in his approach. The main thrust of his coaching philosophy that he expressed while he was seeking the job and once he had it was that he wanted the Steelers to be a tough football team.

"To me, that's what building a winning team was all about. I wanted to run the ball and I wanted to play defense," he said. "I knew you had to score and you had to pass, but toughness mattered at every turn in this game, and it still does. That's what I wanted my teams to be known for above everything else."

Cowher was true to his word from Day One. The Steelers certainly had plenty of toughness and a mean streak during the majority of Chuck Noll's reign as a four-time Super Bowl winner with the Steelers, but they seemed to lose a bit of that identity in his final years with the team.

The Steelers had turned into an ordinary team in Noll's last four years, going 5-11, 9-7, 9-7, and 7-9 from 1988 through 1991 and making the playoffs just once in that span. Cowher gave the team a spark that had been missing. The Steelers went 11-5 and finished first in the AFC Central.

While the roster did not have overwhelming talent—Neil O'Donnell and Bubby Brister handled the QB chores—the Steelers played with an energy and ferocity that had been missing. That regular-season success did not translate to the playoffs, as the Steelers were beaten decisively by the Buffalo Bills 24-3 at Three Rivers Stadium in the divisional playoffs.

The Steelers were a winning team nearly every year in Cowher's coaching regime, and they made the playoffs in his first six seasons at the helm. In 1994, the Steelers went 12-4 and pummeled the Cleveland Browns 29-9 in the divisional playoffs. That gave them the opportunity to win the AFC Championship at home against the San Diego Chargers.

Few thought San Diego had a chance in Pittsburgh in January. The Steelers had a ferocious team that featured Greg Lloyd, Levon Kirkland, and future Hall of Famer Rod Woodson. The Chargers had gotten hot over the second half of the season and featured a journeyman quarterback in Stan Humphries.

The Chargers could only muster three points well into the third quarter, but Humphries persevered and rallied San Diego to a 17-13 victory.

The heartbreak stayed with Cowher for a year, and looked as if it might be repeated in the AFC Championship again the following year.

The Steelers once again hosted that game after a strong 11-5 season and an overwhelming 40-21 win over the Bills in the divisional playoff games. All they had to do to get to their first Super Bowl of the Cowher era was beat the mediocre Indianapolis Colts, who finished the season with a 9-7 record.

The Colts didn't appear to have the talent to compete with the Steelers as they featured Jim Harbaugh at quarterback and a cast of no-names who had played hard for head coach Ted Marchibroda. Harbaugh was an ordinary quarterback throughout his NFL career, finishing with a 66-74-0 record and a 129-117 TD-interception ratio.

However, the Steelers couldn't put them away and were clinging to a 20-16 lead on the game's final play. Harbaugh floated a pass into the end zone that hit wideout Aaron Bailey in the midsection as he fell to the turf. Bailey tried to clutch the ball and keep it from hitting the ground, but he failed by inches. The Steelers had their AFC title and were going to the Super Bowl to take on the powerful Dallas Cowboys.

The Steelers had twice defeated the Cowboys in the Chuck Noll era, but this Cowboys team was not about to let another opportunity slip through their grasp. Dallas had Troy Aikman, Emmitt Smith, and Michael Irvin on the offensive side, and their defense was relentless.

The Cowboys did not play their best game, but they still came away with a 27-17 victory. Cowher was heartbroken with the defeat, but it was a setback that would not derail him.

He would continue to coach in the Steel City until he got back to the Super Bowl and won it.

That would take eleven more years. After getting to the Super Bowl in his fourth season as a head coach, Cowher wouldn't get back there until his 15th, following the 2005 season.

It didn't look like that was a possibility, as the Steelers were 7-5 with four weeks to go and had played inconsistently. But Cowher told his team they were champions and would not lose another game.

His players bought it, as they finished 11-5 and registered road playoff wins over the Cincinnati Bengals, Colts, and Denver Broncos to make it to Super Bowl XL against the Seattle Seahawks.

Cowher may have known he was getting close to the end of his reign in Pittsburgh, but he wasn't telling anyone. However, that was not the case with running back Jerome Bettis. "The Bus" made it clear the 2005 season was his last and that the Super Bowl— which was played in his hometown of Detroit—was to be his last game.

It ended in storybook fashion for Bettis, as the Steelers outlasted the Seahawks 21-10. It was a moment of sheer joy for Cowher, who celebrated tearfully with his family.

Cowher coached one more season and then decided to retire and move on to the television booth after an 8-8 year.

Many have expected Cowher to leave the CBS set and get back to the sidelines, but he has not decided to return to coaching yet.

Whether he does or doesn't make that decision, Cowher still has a legacy that includes 149 regular-season wins, twelve more in the postseason, and one Super Bowl title. Not bad for a former free-agent linebacker and special-teams ace.

For the record

Bill Cowher
Regular-season record: 149-90-1, .623
Postseason record: 12-9, .571
One Super Bowl victory

#26

DAN REEVES

There were few things that Dan Reeves didn't know about coaching by the midway point of his playing career with the Dallas Cowboys. Drafted out of South Carolina as a quarterback, Reeves never had the kind of arm that NFL teams wanted and he was quickly converted to running back.

Tom Landry loved Reeves's versatility because he could run inside, carry the ball on sweeps to the outside, block effectively, and catch passes. He also put his quarterbacking skills on display, as he could throw the option pass, and Landry was never afraid to call on those skills.

But more than simply executing as a player, Reeves learned the game like a coach under Landry and he was able to advise all of his offensive teammates where they were supposed to be on each play if they ever had any questions.

The die was cast when Reeves donned his No. 30 uniform for the Cowboys, and perhaps well before that. Reeves was going to be a football coach someday.

Reeves's knowledge and ability to communicate with his teammates was not lost on Landry. He made Reeves a player-coach in 1971. Eventually, Reeves became a full-time assistant for Landry and he stayed with the Cowboys until the 1981 season.

Reeves had been sought by several NFL teams and had been a legitimate head-coaching candidate, but that year the Denver Broncos came calling and named Reeves as their head coach.

Reeves tried to turn the Broncos into a winning team with the likes of Steve DeBerg and Craig Morton at quarterback. While the Broncos finished with a 10-6 record in 1981—and did not make the playoffs—they slipped back to 2-7 in the strike year of '82.

However, that put the Broncos in a position to obtain rookie quarterback John Elway from the celebrated quarterback Class of 1983.

Elway was actually drafted by the Baltimore Colts, and he had said prior to the draft that he would not play in Baltimore. Unlike most rookies, Elway had leverage since he also was a Major League Baseball prospect and was property of George Steinbrenner of the New York Yankees. When the Colts came to believe that Elway would not relent, they traded his rights to the Broncos.

Reeves and Elway immediately formed a winning combination, even though their relationship was often tempestuous. Elway's remarkable athleticism and awe-inspiring arm strength gave the Broncos a chance to win nearly every game. They finished 9-7 and made the playoffs in 1983, and were 13-3 the following year.

The Broncos were the No. 2 seed in the AFC playoffs behind the Miami Dolphins (14-2) in 1984, and it was expected that the two teams would meet in the AFC Championship game to see who represented the conference in the Super Bowl. However, the Broncos were eliminated in the divisional playoffs by a feisty Pittsburgh Steelers team that took command in the second half and beat the Broncos 24-17.

While the Broncos finished 11-5 in 1985, it would not be good enough to make the playoffs, and there were grumblings about the leadership of Reeves and Elway. It was hard for local fans to understand how this team could fall short of the postseason, and the situation was going to have to change quickly.

The Broncos responded in 1986, as Elway grew more experienced and learned how to finish games. This time an 11-5 record was good enough to win the AFC West title, and the Broncos outlasted the New England Patriots 22-17 in the divisional playoffs, putting Reeves and Elway in the AFC Title game at Cleveland.

The Browns were more than a worthy opponent, and they took a 20-13 lead late in the fourth quarter when Bernie Kosar hit wideout Brian Brennan with a forty-eight-yard touchdown pass. The Broncos botched the ensuing kickoff and had to start their drive from the two-yard line.

What followed was legendary, as Elway led the Broncos downfield with a series of on-the-money passes in the face of a brutal Cleveland pass rush. The Browns had several chances to stop Elway, but could not do it, and the game was propelled into overtime when Elway connected with wideout Mark Jackson on a five-yard touchdown pass in the final moments.

Reeves breathed a sigh of relief, as his quarterback had rescued the team from a most precarious position. The Broncos would complete the comeback when Rich Karlis connected on a field goal in overtime to send the Broncos to Super Bowl XXI against the Giants.

It was a thrilling moment for Reeves as a head coach. He was going into the Super Bowl with a team that had glorious momentum and perhaps the best quarterback in the game. However, the AFC champions would fall short in Super Bowl XXI against the New York Giants because New York quarterback Phil Simms completed 22-of-25 passes and the Giants' defense was simply too strong for Denver's ordinary offensive line. Even though Denver led at halftime, the Giants earned a 39-20 decision.

Losing in the Super Bowl would become a habit for Reeves and Elway. A year later, the Broncos found themselves back in the Super Bowl against the Washington Redskins, and after Denver jumped out to a 10-0 lead, the Redskins roared back with thirty-five second-quarter points and earned a 42-10 blowout win.

Reeves was proving to be a master at navigating the Broncos through the regular season, but they would fall apart in the Super Bowl. The same scenario took place following the 1989 season. The Broncos had a limited running game and an ordinary defense, but they won the AFC again. This time they would meet the San Francisco 49ers in the Super Bowl.

The game turned out to be the most lopsided game in the history of the series. The Niners rode the superb play of Joe Montana and Jerry Rice to a monstrous 55-10 triumph.

Reeves was humiliated by his Super Bowl record, and his relationship with Elway would grow more distant over the ensuing three years.

Elway drew a line in the sand with owner Pat Bowlen about Reeves following an 8-8 finish in 1992, and the owner sided with the quarterback. Reeves was let go and Mike Shanahan came to Denver.

Reeves was hired immediately by general manager George Young of the New York Giants. Reeves had been a candidate for the Giants' head coaching position while he was still an assistant in Dallas, and Young ultimately hired Ray Perkins to coach the team.

This time, there would be no other choice for Young to make. Reeves inherited a team that went 6-10, but he led them to an 11-5 record and a playoff spot in 1993. The Giants defeated the Minnesota Vikings 17-10 in the wild-card game, but got overwhelmed 44-3 by the 49ers.

Reeves could not get back to the playoffs in three more years with New York, and he would coach the Atlanta Falcons in 1998. While Reeves developed a reputation for a lack of creativity on offense in Denver and New York, he proved to be the perfect leader in Atlanta.

The Falcons became the "Dirty Birds" and rolled to a 14-2 record with Chris Chandler at quarterback and Jamal Anderson carrying the load at running back. The Falcons made it to the NFC Championship game at Minnesota, where they were expected to be pounded by the explosive Vikings.

Minnesota had a brilliant passing attack that year and set offensive records with Randall Cunningham at quarterback throwing to Cris Carter and Randy Moss. Reeves's team was not intimidated and pulled off a shocking 30-27 overtime victory.

Ironically, the Falcons met Elway and the Broncos in the Super Bowl. The game proved to be Elway's last as an NFL player, and he directed Denver to a 34-19 win over his former coach's team. Both men had tried to play down the rift in their relationship, but it was a bitter defeat for Reeves.

His Falcons teams would never make it back to the Super Bowl and would only make it to the NFL playoffs once in the next six seasons.

Reeves would end his coaching career after the team went 3-10 in 2003.

Reeves won 190 regular season games during his coaching career, and that's the second-most of any head coach who did not win a championship, trailing only Marty Schottenheimer's mark of 200.

Reeves may never have developed the kind of rapport with Elway that he wanted, but he kept the team focused and winning, and his consistency allowed him to take three teams to the playoffs.

For the record

Dan Reeves
Regular-season record: 190–165–2, .535
Postseason record: 11–9, .550
Four conference championships

#27

ANDY REID

Andy Reid learned his lessons well as an assistant coach in college football. He coached at five schools between 1982 and 1991 before he got his first big break and was called by Mike Holmgren to begin his pro coaching career as a tight ends and offensive line coach with the Packers.

Reid eventually worked his way up to quarterbacks coach in 1997, and he quickly developed a reputation as an up-and-comer while working with Brett Favre. Teams around the NFL started to make inquiries about Reid, and the Packers thought they were protecting themselves when they named Reid as an assistant head coach.

However, that did not stop the Eagles from pursuing him hard prior to the 1999 season. Philadelphia had endured a brutal 1998 season, and the team was lacking in talent at the skill positions and depth at nearly everywhere else.

One of the first moves of the Reid regime was the drafting of quarterback Donovan McNabb in 1999. While the move was not looked at favorably by long-suffering Eagles fans who had wanted the team to draft Texas running back Ricky Williams, McNabb was a smart leader and Reid could teach him the West Coast offense.

The Eagles struggled with a 5-11 record in '99, but Reid had put his system in place and the team was ready to make a move up the standings the next year. The Eagles went 11-5 and won a spot in the playoffs as a wild-card team. The Eagles trounced the Bucs 21-3 in their first playoff game, but they were stopped 20-10 in the divisional playoffs by the Giants.

The Eagles would become a consistent playoff team under Reid, making the postseason five straight years. However, the Eagles seemed to be a limited team, and their weaknesses would usually come to the forefront during the postseason.

While McNabb developed into a solid quarterback who was capable of diagnosing opponents' weaknesses and exploiting them, he did not have a stellar crew of receivers and the running game was not first-rate.

As a result, the Eagles regularly came up short in the NFC Championship game. They were not expected to beat the St. Louis Rams following the 2001 season, but they were favored each of the two following seasons against the Bucs and Panthers.

Even though they had been a dominant team at home, they couldn't use their Veterans Stadium advantage constructively. Both the Bucs and Panthers walked into the Vet and beat the Eagles convincingly.

Just when it looked like the Eagles would never get to the Super Bowl under Reid, they added superstar wideout Terrell Owens prior to the 2004 season and they rolled to an NFC-best 13-3 record.

After beating the Vikings 27-14 in the divisional playoffs, the Eagles found themselves back in the NFC Championship game for the fourth consecutive season. While the atmosphere around Philadelphia was frought with doom and gloom as many pessimistic fans thought they would get stopped short of the Super Bowl once again, the Eagles dominated the Falcons 27-10 and earned a spot in Super Bowl XXXIX against the New England Patriots.

The game was tied 14-14 after three quarters, but when Corey Dillon scored a touchdown and Adam Vinatieri kicked a field goal in the fourth quarter, the Patriots had a ten-point lead and appeared to be in control of the game.

However, McNabb threw a thirty-yard touchdown pass with 1:55 remaining, and the Eagles got the ball back with forty-six seconds remaining. They could not do anything with their final possession and the Patriots were celebrating their third Super Bowl title at the end of the game.

Owens had been a huge factor in the Eagles' improved offense as he caught seventy-seven passes for 1,200 yards and fourteen touchdowns, but he was also a huge divisive factor within the locker room. Owens was the personification of the wide receiver as diva, and he also blamed McNabb for the team's loss in the Super Bowl.

The Eagles became a divided team, and they fell to 6-10 in 2005, before bouncing back with another division title in 2006. Reid knew that his team was starting to get old, and he began to make major changes to the roster.

The Eagles remained a contender and made the playoffs three consecutive years from 2008 through 2010, but they could not maintain that success and the Eagles slipped to 8-8 in 2011 before capitulating with a 4-12 season the following year.

The 2012 season was particularly brutal for Reid, as his oldest son, Garrett, died of a heroin overdose during the Eagles' training camp. Reid tried to carry on, but his team was no longer responding to him. The Eagles fired Reid after that painful season.

Many thought that he would remain on the sidelines for at least a full season so he could address his personal loss and take stock of his career. But Reid wanted no part of that. The Kansas City Chiefs had an opening, and when they offered him the head coaching position, he accepted it willingly.

Reid acquired quarterback Alex Smith, instituted a powerful running game, and the Chiefs went 11-5 and went to the playoffs as a wild-card team. The Chiefs built a 38-10 lead on the road over the Indianapolis Colts, but the defense fell apart and Kansas City ended up dropping a 45-44 decision.

The Chiefs remained competitive in 2014 with a 9-7 record, but losses to the Tennessee Titans in the opener and the Oakland Raiders in mid-November ruined their playoff chances.

Still, Reid has re-established himself as one of the best coaches in the game, and he demonstrated that he still has one of the best offensive minds in the business.

He has made just one Super Bowl appearance and his team lost that game, but his teams have won consistently and he has regularly been able to out-scheme opposing coaches. That's not likely to change any time soon.

For the record

Andy Reid
Regular-season record: 150-105-1, .588
Postseason record: 10-10, .500

#28

CURLY LAMBEAU

There's only one reason an NFL franchise was given to the Northern Wisconsin hamlet of Green Bay. It was due to the strength, skill, persistence, and desire of one Earl L. "Curly" Lambeau.

Lambeau was the head coach of the Packers from 1921 through 1949, but in addition to leading them on the sidelines for more than three decades, he founded the franchise, played for the Packers, got backing for them when times were tough, and helped them win championships.

Lambeau grew up in Green Bay and was a high school football star. He played college football at Wisconsin and Notre Dame, but he had to leave both schools because he had to work at his father's construction business.

Lambeau continued to play football while working at the family business, and in 1921 he urged the Green Bay football team to apply for membership to the American Professional Football Association. That organization was the forerunner to the NFL, and they accepted Green Bay as a member team.

The club got backing from the Indian Packing Company, which was soon taken over by the Acme Packing Company. However, when Acme decided to pull out of its sponsorship, it was left to Lambeau to keep the operation running.

He did so with the help of *Green Bay Press-Gazette* sportswriter George Calhoun and *Press-Gazette* publisher Andrew Turnbull. Calhoun helped publicize the team and raised money to keep it running, while Turnbull came up with the idea and executed a stock sale that allowed locals to buy stakes in the team.

Lambeau became the team's star player and its coach during the 1920s. He threw 24 touchdown passes during his playing career, which was an impressive total at that time. He also came up with the plays, organized the team, and decided which players would be on the field and who would come in as a substitute.

The Packers won regularly during the early years of the league, and they earned three consecutive NFL championships between 1929 and 1931. In those days, there were no playoffs or even a championship game. The Packers simply became league champions because they had the best record during the regular season.

Those championship teams were led by Cal Hubbard, Johnny Blood, and Mike Michalske. The Packers returned to championship form when they signed a slick wide receiver from Alabama named Don Hutson.

Hutson came aboard in 1935, and the Packers won their fourth NFL title a year later. Green Bay had a 10-1-1 record that season, and won the NFL's West Division. They traveled east to play the Boston Redskins in the NFL Championship game. When the Redskins could not sell enough tickets to the game in Boston, it was moved to New York City's Polo Grounds. Nearly 30,000 fans saw Lambeau's Packers trounce the Redskins 21-6.

Arnie Herber threw two touchdown passes in that game, and one of them was to Hutson, who caught five passes for seventy-six yards. Lambeau had built one of the first modern offenses; his team was as efficient as any team in pro football at the passing game.

The Packers made it back to the NFL title game in 1938, but this time they lost to the New York Giants by a 23-17 margin. The following year, the Packers rolled to a 9-2 record to win the West, and they got their revenge on the Giants by beating them 27-0 in the championship game.

That gave Lambeau five championships for his career, and he won one more following the 1944 season when they had an 8-2 regular season record and then beat the Giants 14-7 in the championship game.

Six NFL titles put Lambeau in a tie with George Halas for the most championships won in a career. Halas and Lambeau appeared to be bitter rivals on the field, and both had curmudgeonly personalities off of it. The two men never shook hands in the middle of the field after any Packers-Bears game, but when the Packers needed money for their new City Stadium, it was Halas who helped them raise the funds. That act was indicative of the true respect between the two legendary coaches.

Lambeau was an innovative head coach who initiated the idea of leading his team in daily practice sessions to prepare for each upcoming game. Lambeau also used movie cameras to film games, so his teams could see their mistakes and then work on them in the practice sessions.

Lambeau was a driven man as a coach, and he would push his players hard in their practice sessions and games. He did not care at all if his players liked him; he simply wanted them to be winning football players. He was known as the "Bellicose Belgian" because he yelled at his players with such alarming frequency.

But Lambeau did win games. He had twenty-six winning seasons as head coach during his first twenty-seven years with the Packers, and that's clearly a record that no modern coach will ever get close to.

He struggled in his final two years with the Packers as he was slow to change his ways. His teams stuck with the Single-Wing formation long after the T-formation became standard in the NFL. As a result his team had losing records in 1947 and '48, which was his last season in Green Bay.

Lambeau moved on to become the coach of the Chicago Cardinals for two years, and followed that by coaching the Washington Redskins for two years.

He had a winning 6-5-1 record in his final season as a head coach in 1953. However, his most notable activity in Washington was getting into a shoving match with owner George Preston Marshall that left his players laughing in celebration.

As the years went by, the Packers struggled badly without him, and he was angling to return in the late 1950s. However, when Green Bay hired New York Giants assistant coach Vince Lombardi in 1959, that was the end of Lambeau's coaching career.

It was Lombardi's name that would become synonymous with the franchise. However, the Packers never would have existed in the first place or survived their rocky early years if not for the strength and drive of Lambeau.

For the record

Curly Lambeau
Hall of Fame, 1963
Regular-season record: 226-132-22, .631
Postseason record: 3-2, .600
Six NFL championships

#29

JIM MORA

He may be best known for a viral video that includes his incredulous facial when asked a question about his team's chance of gaining a spot in the playoffs, but Jim Mora's coaching career is worthy of recognition even though his success in the postseason was non-existent.

Mora got his start in coaching at Stanford under head coach John Ralston, and that came after a three-year stint in the Marines. Ralston was struck by Mora's command and drive, and he said he had the "executive ability to run General Motors. He's highly intelligent, disciplined, and with a great grasp of what it takes to succeed."

Mora quickly moved through the college ranks and became an NFL assistant coach with the Seattle Seahawks and the New England Patriots. He moved on to the head coaching ranks when the United States Football League opened its doors in 1982, and he signed on with the Philadelphia Stars.

While the new league had an array of problems, many scouts were impressed with the talent level in the new league, and there were quite a few competitive franchises. The best of them was Mora's Stars, who made it to the championship game in all three years of the league's existence, winning the title in two of those years.

When the league went out of business, the NFL snatched up its top players like Herschel Walker, Jim Kelly, and Reggie White quickly. Mora had also made a name for himself in the USFL, and he was a hot coaching commodity.

The New Orleans Saints came calling, because they had never had a winning season in their history, and they were hoping that Mora could change that. General manager Jim Finks was impressed by Mora's straightforward approach and he had confidence that the coach could turn around the Saints' losing history.

The Saints finished 7-9 in 1986, but there was a big difference between how the team went about its business from the previous year. There was greater discipline and organization, and it seemed like a sense of confidence was developing.

The Saints were an energized and talented team in 1987, and Mora's crew finished with a 12-3-0 record, and that gave the franchise a second-place finish in the NFC West. It also earned the team its first playoff appearance.

It was a remarkable year for the franchise because the success was sudden and explosive. The Saints were just 3-3 after their first six games, and their third loss was a 24-22 decision to the 49ers that featured a disappointing comeback that fell just short.

But the Saints would not lose another game in the regular season, as they reeled off nine straight wins behind the accurate passing of USFL refugee and Cajun native Bobby Hebert, the running of Dalton Hilliard and Rueben Mayes, and the receiving of Eric Martin and a glue-fingered tight end named Hoby Brenner.

While none of those players were All-Pros, they functioned at an efficient level under Mora's leadership. Hebert did not have a strong arm, but he was an accurate short- and medium-range passer and he got the ball away quickly.

The defense was the backbone of the 1987 Saints, and it featured linebackers Rickey Jackson, Pat Swilling, Vaughan Johnson, and Sam Mills. Many NFL observers thought Jackson was the second-best linebacker in the NFL behind Lawrence Taylor of the New York Giants, and the foursome was almost certainly the best in the league.

The Saints announced their presence among the NFL's elite when they went on the road in November and beat the Los Angeles Rams and 49ers, and then came home and defeated the defending champion New York Giants.

Many thought the red-hot Saints would be the team to beat as the playoffs got underway, and they were cocky favorites when they hosted the 8-7 Minnesota Vikings in the wild-card round of the playoffs.

The Saints started the game in impressive fashion when Hebert hit Martin with a ten-yard touchdown pass in the first quarter, but the Vikings scored forty-four of the next forty-seven points to humble them in the Superdome.

The defeat stung Mora and his players, and while the Saints posted a winning record each of the next two years, they did not make it back to the playoffs.

They were an ordinary 8-8 in 1990, but that record was good enough for them to grab the final wild-card spot in the playoffs. This time, Mora's crew was forced to play at Chicago against Mike Ditka's veteran Bears, and the Saints could not contend with the twenty-one-degree temperature and dropped a 16-6 decision.

The Saints returned to the playoffs in '91 after winning the NFC West with an 11-5-0 record, but they were upset at home by the Atlanta Falcons.

Mora and his Saints made it to the postseason again the following year, and they appeared to have a chance to finally win a game when they hosted the Philadelphia Eagles. The Saints led the game 17-7 at halftime, and when superb placekicker Morten Andersen added a forty-two-yard field goal early in the third quarter, the Superdome fans were raucous and let the visiting Eagles hear it.

However, the Eagles had a pass rush that included Hall of Famer Reggie White and running mate Jerome Brown. They turned up the intensity and punished Hebert throughout the second half with a vicious pass rush, and the Eagles outscored them 26-0 in the fourth quarter and rolled to a 36-20 victory.

Mora and his team never got over that defeat. He would remain with New Orleans for four more seasons, but their talent level and confidence eroded over that period.

Mora left the Saints following the 1996 season and after spending a year away from the sidelines, he was named head coach of the Indianapolis Colts in 1998.

The Colts had drafted quarterback Peyton Manning that year, and they struggled to a 3-13 record. However, they turned that around the following season and went 13-3 to earn first place in the AFC East. The Colts had a home playoff game against the Tennessee Titans, and they could not contend with Titans running back Eddie George, who gashed the Indianapolis defense for 162 yards. The Colts dropped a 19-16 decision.

It seemed like Mora would finally get his playoff victory the following year. The Colts made the postseason as a wild-card team with a 10-6 record. They played a near-perfect road game against the Dolphins, and took a 17-10 fourth quarter lead when placekicker Mike Vanderjagt boomed home a fifty-yard field goal with 5:01 remaining.

The Indianapolis defense had been strong throughout the game, but it gave up the game-tying touchdown with forty seconds remaining, and the two teams went to overtime. Vanderjagt had a chance to win the game with a forty-nine-yard attempt in overtime, but he could not convert, and the Dolphins won the game on a seventeen-yard touchdown run by Lamar Smith.

That defeat was the last of Mora's six attempts to win postseason games, and his team had failed in all of them. He never made excuses and he always assessed his team openly and honestly when mistakes were made. He took responsibility for his own issues and never tried to excuse them.

His blunt assessments and pronouncements were often captured on camera. He spared no one, including the media. "You think you know, but you don't know. And you never will."

His famous "playoffs" rant remains popular on football broadcasts and YouTube.

Mora had taken struggling teams in New Orleans and Indianapolis and turned them into consistent regular-season winners, but that's where it ended. He was not able to succeed in the playoffs, and those defeats are part of his legacy.

However, if he had not been such a competent and strong-willed coach, the Saints and Colts would have taken much longer to become successful teams.

For the record

> **Jim Mora**
> Regular-season record: 125–106–0, .541
> Postseason record: 0–6, .000
> Two division championships

#30

JOHN FOX

J ohn Fox may coach in the modern era of professional football, but he does it with a mentality that would make coaches from older eras like Vince Lombardi, Don Shula, and Chuck Noll smile broadly.

Fox has a conservative outlook to his game, and he wants to take care of the basics whenever he has been put in charge of a team. He wants his team to run the ball. He wants his team to stop the run. He wants his team to pressure the opponent's quarterback.

Do all three of those things, Fox believes, and your team is going to win a lot more games than it loses.

John Fox

Fox never played professional football, but he was a hard enough hitter in the San Diego State secondary during his college days to earn the nickname "Crash."

He started his coaching career shortly thereafter, and it's no surprise that a guy who loved to deliver the big hit would gravitate towards coaching defense. That would eventually become his specialty, and he had a long run as a college assistant coach until Noll plucked him to coach the Pittsburgh Steelers' defensive backs in 1989. After spending three years with the Steelers, he moved on to the Chargers and coached two years under Bobby Ross.

By that time, Fox had earned a reputation as one of the sharpest defensive coaches in the league, and Oakland Raiders head coach Art Shell hired him to be the team's defensive coordinator. His tenure with the Raiders was a short one, because Fox saw how things operated within the franchise.

Owner Al Davis was still a man of great influence, and he did not hesitate to tell Raiders' coaches what he thought of their game plans and what changes needed to be made. Fox did not see this as one of the game's most innovative minds offering up his knowledge. Instead, he saw Davis as the worst kind of meddler and he abruptly quit because he simply couldn't abide it.

That decision may fly in the face of Fox's general perception from the image he has projected because he seems like such a likable and agreeable individual. However, dealing with an owner who wouldn't let coaches do what they were paid to do rubbed Fox the wrong way and he stood by his principles.

The New York Giants took notice, and they hired him as their defensive coordinator. He got consistent results, as the Giants finished in the top 10 in points allowed in each of his five seasons there.

The Giants won the 2000 NFC Championship, as they ripped the Minnesota Vikings 41-0 in the conference championship game, and Fox earned a great deal of credit for the way his defense shut down what had been a very explosive Minnesota offense.

While the Giants were obliterated by the Baltimore Ravens in the Super Bowl, Fox had established his reputation as one of the top defensive coordinators in the NFL. It would be just a matter of time until he got an opportunity to become an NFL head coach.

That chance came in 2002, when the moribund Carolina Panthers hired him to make immediate repairs on a team that had finished a dreadful 1-15 the previous year under George Seifert, and looked hopeless.

Fox changed that immediately, as the Panthers became a respectable team and finished 7-9. Fox was not a complex head coach who came up with game plans that were designed to force opposing coaches into mental gymnastics. He merely wanted both of his lines to win the battle in the trenches and he wanted his running game to exert his will on opponents.

The Panthers not only played respectable football in 2002, but they also established a reputation for toughness, and the holdover who had suffered through the dreadful 2001 performance were believers. The 2003 season saw the Panthers get off to a shocking 8-2 start, as the offense had a versatile attack with quarterback Jake Delhomme, running back Stephen Davis, and wide receivers Steve Smith and Muhsin Muhammad.

While the offense moved the ball consistently, the defense often locked down opponents and made big plays at key moments.

They finished first in the NFC South Division and beat the Cowboys by a convincing 29-10 in the wild-card round of the playoffs. Despite that victory, they were not expected to give the explosive St. Louis Rams much of a battle in the divisional playoffs on the road. Instead, the Panthers extended the game to double overtime, and they beat the Rams when Delhomme hit the explosive Smith with a sixty-nine-yard game-winning touchdown pass.

The Panthers pulled off another upset in the NFC Championship game when they punished the Philadelphia Eagles 14-3 on the road, and that gave Fox an opportunity to take his team to the Super Bowl in his second season.

Carolina had a daunting task in trying to beat the New England Patriots, but they stayed in the game for sixty minutes and tied the score when Ricky Proehl caught a game-tying touchdown pass from Delhomme with 1:14 remaining. However, Fox's dreams of glory dissolved into teams when Adam Vinatieri hit a game-winning forty-one-yard field goal.

Two years later, the Panthers made it back to the NFC Championship game, but they lost an opportunity to get back to the Super Bowl when they dropped a 34-14 decision to the Seattle Seahawks.

Fox kept the Panthers competitive through the 2009 season, but they fell apart in 2010 and Fox was fired after Carolina slipped to 2-14.

The Denver Broncos wasted no time in hiring him, and even though they had a substandard offense and an ordinary defense, they made the playoffs in 2011 as they won a very poor AFC West with an 8-8 record. Most expected a blowout in their playoff game against the Steelers, but quarterback Tim Tebow threw a game-winning touchdown pass in overtime to shock Pittsburgh.

There would be no magic the following week at New England, and neither Fox nor general manager John Elway had any belief that Tebow was a viable alternative at quarterback.

The Broncos made a bold move and signed Peyton Manning in free agency, and even though he was coming off neck surgery that caused him to miss the 2011 season, the Broncos turned over their offense to him.

The results were spectacular, as the Broncos went 13-3, 13-3, and 12-4 over the next three seasons. They parlayed their explosive offense and hard-hitting defense into a Super Bowl appearance following the 2013 season, but the Broncos played poorly in the championship game and were blown out by the Seahawks.

When Denver lost its divisional playoff game the following year at home against the Indianapolis Colts, the Broncos and Fox decided to part company. While Elway announced the decision as mutual, there were behind-the-scenes disagreements between Fox and Manning as well as Fox and Elway that led to the change.

Fox was pursued immediately by a Chicago Bears team that played pitiful football in 2014. They took a look at Fox's track record and saw how successful he had been when he took over a brutal team in Carolina, and believed he was the right man for the job. He was hired by Chicago days after leaving Denver.

Fox knows how to coach defense, eliminate errors, and find a way to win. While he may have fallen short of winning the Super Bowl, he has the ability to get the most out of a team and the Bears are counting on him to return them to respectability.

For the record

> **John Fox**
> Regular-season record: 119-89-0, .572
> Postseason record: 8-7, .533

#31

GEORGE SEIFERT

Do you know who Phil Bengtson was?

Even some of the most devout, long-time (non-Green Bay Packers) fans have no idea who Bengtson was or what he did.

But he has a page in the history of pro football and even his own chapter in the Packers' lengthy history. When Vince Lombardi decided to retire from his position as head coach of the Green Bay Packers, Bengtson was named to take over.

While the Packers were starting to get older, many thought Bengtson would merely take the handoff from Lombardi and the team would continue to contend for championships.

But running a championship team is not easy, and the Packers quickly became also-rans.

George Seifert could have been to the Niners what Bengtson was to the Packers—a footnote in team history—following head coach Bill Walsh's retirement.

Walsh was the genius who had been the architect of the Niners' rise to prominence. They couldn't possibly succeed without him. How could the quiet and expressionless Seifert follow one of the greatest and most inventive coaches in the history of the game?

Here's what Seifert did. He coached the 49ers for eight seasons, and he won double-digit games in all of them. He won the Super Bowl in his first year as head coach and he won it again five years later. He had a regular season record of 114-62-0 with the Niners and his teams won six NFC West championships.

But when most people think of the game's greatest coaches, Seifert doesn't even get a sniff.

It's time for them to think again.

Seifert may not have been a genius like his predecessor, but he was a perfectionist with the 49ers. He had started with Walsh as his secondary coach in 1980, and a year later he had three rookies starting in the defensive backfield when the Niners won their first Super Bowl

Three years later, he was named the Niners' defensive coordinator. The 49ers would go on to win their second championship of the Walsh era following the 1984 season as they rolled to a 15-1 record and hammered the Miami Dolphins in the Super Bowl.

However, Joe Montana and the Niners offense were not unscathed that season. During practice every day, Walsh's offense would go up against Seifert's defense. Seifert's defense often got the best of those battles.

When Walsh stepped down following the Niners' heart-stopping victory over the Cincinnati Bengals in Super Bowl XXIII, there was an air of a letdown surrounding San Francisco. The story of

Bengtson was a bit fresher in 1989 than it is now, and most expected that Seifert did not have the coaching skill or personality to follow Walsh.

Some of those thoughts came from Walsh. He respected Seifert and knew he was a good coach, but he wanted to protect his own legacy. Walsh had many insecurities, and he was not above raising questions about his successor.

Many picked up on Walsh's thoughts and questioned Seifert's overall ability. Seifert was well aware of the whispering campaign.

"There was no way I couldn't be aware of it," Seifert said. "There were a lot of things being said, but I concentrated on coaching the team and preparing for each game as much as I could. I developed the most as a coach under Bill. I have always held him in the highest regard."

Seifert clearly took the high road.

He may not have shown it on the sidelines, but Seifert knew how to coach football. For one thing, he raised the morale inside the 49ers locker room.

The players were used to the regal Walsh, and his uncommunicative ways. Walsh would talk to players he perceived as his leaders, but he would often ignore many others.

Seifert talked to everyone and let them know his expectations and where they stood. He might not have been cracking jokes and he might not have been the players' buddy, but he let them know in an honest fashion where they stood with him.

Seifert came in with a spectacular 14-2 season, and the 49ers were even better that year in the postseason. They dominated the Minnesota Vikings 41-13 and then punished the Los Angeles Rams 30-3 in the NFC Championship game.

They continued their mission of destruction in Super Bowl XXIV against John Elway and the Denver Broncos. The Niners scored two touchdowns in every quarter and they pounded the Broncos 55-10 in the most one-sided game in Super Bowl history.

As well as Montana played throughout the 1989 season, he was nearing the end of his time with the 49ers. When Montana was seriously injured in the 1990 NFC Championship game against the Giants, Seifert knew that it was time to turn the team over to Steve Young on a full-time basis.

There was no controversy at first, because Montana was not healthy enough to play in the 1991 season, but when he came back in 1992, Montana's supporters barked their support.

Seifert was strong enough not to make a move. Young remained as a starter, and Montana would be traded to the Kansas City Chiefs after the '92 season.

A weak coach would not have been able to stick to his guns. But Seifert knew that Young was a brilliant quarterback in his own right and he was just coming into his own.

Young would lead the Niners to one of their best seasons in 1994. They rolled to yet another NFC West crown with a 13-3 record, and were an unstoppable force during the playoffs.

San Francisco humiliated the Chicago Bears 44-15 in the divisional playoffs, and that set up a confrontation with the defending Super Bowl champion Dallas Cowboys in the NFC Championship.

This may have been the most worthy team the 49ers faced in their championship years, but they did not let this game get away. They rolled to a 38-28 victory as Young's passing and the 49ers' active defense frustrated the Cowboys at every turn.

Another Super Bowl appearance would prove fruitful for Seifert and Young. The upstart San Diego Chargers had shocked the football world by beating the marauding Pittsburgh Steelers in the AFC title game, and some thought of Bobby Ross's Chargers as a team of destiny.

That title disappeared in the early moments of the first quarter. The Niners scored two touchdowns before the game was five minutes old and rolled to a 49-26 victory.

Young threw a record six touchdown passes in the win and famously wrestled the monkey off of his back. Prior to that win, many critics said Young simply could not win "the big one." He ended that reputation in remarkable fashion.

Seifert coached two more seasons with the Niners, and went 11-5 and 12-4 in those seasons. However, the Niners did not want him around any longer and he resigned, as the organization had been giving him the cold shoulder.

He would return to coaching in 1999 with the Carolina Panthers, and after two non-descript seasons, he had a brutal 1-15 year in 2001 to close his career.

It was a tough way to go out, but it doesn't change the fact that Seifert was one of thirteen NFL coaches to win multiple Super Bowls and have eight seasons in which he won ten or more games.

He may have been in a good position to work under Walsh for so many years, but he established his own legacy as a brilliant defensive mind and one of the game's best coaches.

For the record

> **George Seifert**
> Regular-season record: 114-62-0, .648
> Postseason record: 10-5, .667
> Two Super Bowl victories

161

#32

JON GRUDEN

To many NFL fans, Jon Gruden is the pointed analyst on *Monday Night Football* who has a tendency to go to extremes when describing plays on an every-week basis. "This Peyton Manning, this Tom Brady, this Philip Rivers, this Cam Newton … this Ryan Fitzpatrick …"

… According to Gruden, they are all the greatest.

While he is fairly accomplished at breaking down plays, and slightly palatable since he stopped fighting for air time with Ron Jaworski, it's easy to pick up on the fact that this former coach would like to be back on the sidelines.

Jon Gruden

Gruden has certainly been through the wars and created an even bigger impression when he was on the sidelines for the Oakland Raiders and the Tampa Bay Buccaneers. He nearly took the Raiders all the way to the Super Bowl, and he got there with the Bucs and led them to their only championship.

But that's more the climax of the story. Gruden started his NFL coaching career with the San Francisco 49ers in 1990. Mike Holmgren, who was the offensive coordinator under George Seifert, hired Gruden as a quality control assistant.

With that one year of experience, Gruden was able to get an assistant coaching job at the University of Pittsburgh. From there, it was back to the NFL and Holmgren when he was named head coach of the Green Bay Packers in 1992. After working with Brett Favre as the Packers' quarterback coach, Gruden took an offensive coordinator position with the Philadelphia Eagles in 1995.

While the Eagles did not have stellar offensive personnel—Ty Detmer and Rodney Peete shared the quarterback duties—Gruden built one of the top offenses in the league. Many around the league took notice, including Raiders owner Al Davis.

Gruden, a practitioner of the West Coast Offense, was hired by Davis to coach the Raiders. Davis had long favored using an offense that featured a downfield passing attack, but his team had been struggling and backsliding, so he gave Gruden the chance to build his own attack in an attempt to raise the Raiders' level of play.

Gruden quickly became known around the league for his quirkiness and sideline antics. In a league where many coaches worked long hours so they could figure out opponents' tendencies and build a winning strategy, Gruden decided he was going to get a jump on the competition by coming in to work at 4 a.m. Gruden made it a point to let everyone know how early he was arriving, and the media soon picked up on it.

He also had a tendency to make strange faces on the sidelines when referees' calls went against the Raiders or one of his players made a mistake. His facial contortions and diminutive stature appeared to have an odd resemblance to the wooden doll character "Chucky" from the fright movie *Child's Play*. Thereafter, Gruden was regularly referred to as Chucky in a demeaning way.

While Gruden did not embrace the nickname, he slowly built the Raiders into one of the better teams in the league, and that eased the pressure that Davis put on him.

The Raiders were 8-8 in Gruden's first two seasons, but the 2000 Raiders turned the corner and went 12-4, finishing first in the AFC West. With Rich Gannon handling the quarterback duties, the Raiders completely eschewed Davis's downfield passing game and became an effective West Coast team.

The Raiders won seven of eight games in the middle of the season, and that included back-to-back road victories over the 49ers and the Kansas City Chiefs. Nothing made Davis happier than beating his cross-bay rivals and then his team's traditional AFL rival.

The Raiders rolled into the playoffs with a head of steam and easily dispatched the Miami Dolphins 27-0. The ease of that victory made them favorites over the Baltimore Ravens in the AFC title game, but the Baltimore defense was playing at the highest level the NFL had seen since the 1985 Chicago Bears, and they came into Oakland and squashed the Raiders 16-3.

The Raiders were solid again in 2001, and defended their AFC West title. After beating the New York Jets in the wild-card game, they earned a date with the New England Patriots in the divisional playoffs. The Raiders seemed to have that game locked up when Raiders defensive back Charles Woodson forced a late fumble from Tom Brady, which gave the Raiders the ball in the final moments.

Since the Raiders had a 13-10 lead at the time, it appeared all they would have to do was run a few plays and grind out the final moments. But before that could happen, the officials got together and decided Brady's arm was coming forwards as he fumbled and the officials determined this to be a "tucking" motion, which made it an incomplete pass.

The Pats held on to the ball, and placekicker Adam Vinatieri kicked the tying field goal and then won the game with another three-pointer in overtime. The game, played in a New England snowstorm, became one of the most legendary NFL games ever played.

It would also be the last game Gruden would ever coach for the Raiders. After the back-to-back seasons, Gruden wanted a substantial raise, and Davis was not about to give it to him. He actually traded Gruden to the Tampa Bay Bucs for two first-round draft choices, two second-round picks, and $8 million.

Gruden was taking over a Tampa Bay team that had perhaps the best defense in the league at the time. What they didn't have was a competent offense, and that's why they went after Gruden.

It turned out to be a brilliant move. Gruden found a solid quarterback in Brad Johnson, and he turned the Bucs into a competent offensive team. They went 12-4 and won the NFC South Division.

Still, few thought they would be able to accomplish much in the playoffs. The Bucs and Gruden didn't care about what outsiders thought. They were peaking as the playoffs got underway, and they overpowered the San Francisco 49ers 31-6 and then went to Philadelphia to play Andy Reid's Eagles in the NFC Championship game.

At the time, the Bucs had never won a game in their history when temperatures were below the freezing mark at 32 degrees. Few expected that to change in Philadelphia, where they were forced to play in 20-degree conditions.

After the Eagles scored the first touchdown, it appeared the Bucs would offer little competition. But they stiffened and outscored the Eagles 27-3 the rest of the way and earned a spot in Super Bowl XXXVII against none other than the Raiders.

On paper, it looked like a fairly even matchup, with the Raiders having the better offense and the Bucs having the better defense. However, Gruden gave the Bucs a huge strategic advantage. He knew the Raiders so well that he could advise his defense of each player's tendencies down to the smallest detail. In practice prior to the game, Gruden played the role of Gannon and showed the Raiders how he tended to look to his right and pass to his left, or look to his left and pass to his right on a play called Sluggo Seam.

Additionally, Gannon would pat the ball with his left hand an instant before he got rid of it.

This intimate knowledge of the opposition left the Bucs with overwhelming confidence. They played like it and rolled over the Raiders 48-21 in the game. The Bucs' defense knew Gannon so well that they returned three interceptions for touchdowns in the game.

After that brilliant first year in Tampa, Gruden was unable to match that performance again. They experienced just two more playoff appearances in the next six years, and Gruden was fired after the 2008 season.

He has enjoyed a high profile as the Monday night expert analyst, but Gruden still has a desire to coach again if he can find the right situation. His name is often rumored to be in consideration for head coaching openings, but he has not gone back into the battle since his last season in Tampa.

For the record

Jon Gruden
Regular-season record: 95-81-0, .540
Postseason record: 5-4, .556
One Super Bowl victory

#33

MIKE McCARTHY

It was all right there, so close that Mike McCarthy and his Green Bay Packers could reach out and touch it. Then it all disappeared with a harshness and suddenness that will leave lifetime scars.

The Packers had the defending Super Bowl champion Seattle Seahawks all but beaten in the final moments of the 2014 NFC Championship game, and when Morgan Burnett intercepted a Russell Wilson pass with 5:13 remaining in the fourth quarter with the Packers holding a 19-7 lead, the high fives and congratulatory looks and handshakes began on the Green Bay sideline.

They shouldn't have, because the Packers breathed life into the Seahawks from the point that Burnett wrapped his hands around the ball.

McCarthy deserved his share of the blame, because the Packers were playing conservative football throughout much of the fourth quarter even though they were at their best when attacking with Aaron Rodgers at the quarterback slot.

As the game disintegrated and the Seahawks came back to win the game in overtime, McCarthy and his players wore stunned looks that belied the team's humiliation. No matter what happens in the future, the Packers will long feel the pain of the opportunity they let slip away in 2014.

While it will always hurt, McCarthy has proved to be one of the best coaches of his generation and deserves credit for being one of the best offensive minds in the game.

McCarthy paid his dues as a college assistant and got his first chance to work in the NFL as an assistant on Marty Schottenheimer's Kansas City Chiefs. From there he moved on to Green Bay, New Orleans, and San Francisco, and it was with the Saints that he showed he had the kind of offensive knowledge and teaching ability that would make him an excellent head coach.

Prior to the 2000 season, his first in New Orleans, McCarthy urged the Saints to pick up third-string quarterback Aaron Brooks. Under McCarthy's tutelage, Brooks became a starter and the Saints won the NFC South and a wild-card playoff game. McCarthy won assistant coach of the year honors for his ability to guide Brooks and help him develop into a winning and competitive quarterback.

McCarthy was on the head coaching radar after that, and his chance came in 2006. There were questions in Green Bay, where fans wanted an established winner, but general manager Ted Thompson was convinced that McCarthy had the personal skills as well as the X's and O's knowledge to lead the Packers back to glory.

McCarthy produced immediate results, as he helped the Packers improve from 4-12 in 2005 to 8-8 in his first year.

Green Bay came roaring out of the gate in 2007, and rolled to a 13-3 record. That allowed them to claim the No. 2 seed in the NFC, and they defeated the Seahawks 42-20 in the divisional playoffs.

Since the top-seeded Dallas Cowboys had lost their divisional playoff game to the Giants, the Packers were able to host New York in the NFC title game. It looked like Green Bay and quarterback Brett Favre would earn a trip to the Super Bowl, but the long-time Packer legend's last pass in overtime was intercepted and set the Giants up for the game-winning field goal.

That play began an important trial for McCarthy and Thompson. By the end of the season, they were convinced that they wanted Rodgers to take over at quarterback and that it was time for Favre to retire (preferably) or move on.

Favre began a retirement dance that would go on for several years, but McCarthy and Thompson never wavered. They ultimately let Favre go so he could continue his career with the New York Jets (and then the Minnesota Vikings), and that gave Rodgers the opportunity to take over as the starting quarterback.

While Favre had become the greatest quarterback in Green Bay history and one of the legendary franchise's most beloved icons, McCarthy, Thompson, and Rodgers were ultimately able to win the public relations battle in the eyes of the public because they never vacillated, while Favre seemed to behave like a diva.

Ultimately, Rodgers would prove to be every bit as effective as Favre, and he gave the Packers sensational accuracy and leadership.

Green Bay struggled to a 6-10 record in 2008, but rebounded to 11-5 the following season and that allowed McCarthy's team to make the playoffs. It ended in shocking fashion, as the Packers went up and down the field but lost a 51-45 decision in overtime to Arizona when Rodgers lost a fumble and Cardinals linebacker

Karlos Dansby picked up the loose ball and returned it 17 yards for a game-winning touchdown.

The 2010 season would have a much better finish for McCarthy and the Packers. While they needed a Week 17 win over the Chicago Bears to earn a wild-card spot, they took advantage of that magical opportunity to go on a brilliant postseason run.

They defeated the Eagles, Falcons, and Bears on the road, and earned a spot in Super Bowl XLV against the Pittsburgh Steelers. Rodgers and the Packers built a solid 21-3 lead late in the second quarter and held on to record a 31-25 victory.

The partnership of McCarthy and Rodgers had won as many Super Bowls for Green Bay as Favre had during his legendary run, and the feeling was that Rodgers would continue to improve under McCarthy's tutelage.

McCarthy was able to continue his advanced teaching with Rodgers, and the quarterback became an artist with the football in his hands.

Rodgers developed the best footwork in the league and his passes were more precise than any other quarterback.

While the Packers regularly struggled on the defensive side of the ball, it was clear that nobody wanted to get into shootouts with Green Bay. That included New England QB Tom Brady, who played a brilliant game in Week 13 of the 2014 season, but came up on the short end of a 26-21 loss at Green Bay because Rodgers was even better.

That's one of the reasons that NFC Championship loss to Seattle was so painful for McCarthy and the Packers. Green Bay had already beaten New England in the regular season, and the team had full confidence it could do it again in the Super Bowl.

That would have given McCarthy his second Lombardi Trophy as a head coach, which would have put him in rare company.

However, he still has built a solid career that still appeared to be in its prime as the 2014 season came to an end.

For the record

> **Mike McCarthy**
> Regular-season record: 94–49–1, .666
> Postseason record: 7–6, .538
> One Super Bowl victory

#34

STEVE OWEN

The New York Giants have been one of the NFL's bedrock franchises for decades, and they have cultivated a certain image that has stayed with them most of their successful years.

They play rock-hard defense, they run the ball, and they don't make a lot of mistakes. They play simplistic football, yes, but effective football nonetheless. This was the game plan followed by long-time head coach Steve Owen, who headed the Giants from 1931 through 1953, and 17 of those 23 seasons were winning ones.

Owen gave the Giants franchise consistency and an identity, something that was lacking when he came aboard.

The Giants were a winning team when owner Tim Mara hired him, but there was a mutiny brewing because the players couldn't stand head coach Leroy Andrews. They revolted, went to Mara, and said they couldn't play for the intractable Andrews any longer and the owner went along.

He gave the position to Owen, and he did so with the marching orders that the infighting would stop. Mara was not worried about the Giants' performance on the field because he could see that he had a talented roster. He wanted a coach who would treat his players like men, listen to their issues, and then figure out a way to fix problems. He was sick and tired of players coming upstairs and bothering him. He wanted a coach who could command the locker room with respect.

That's what he got with Owen, who was tough-minded but reasonable throughout the majority of his years with the Giants.

He was also a devotee of defensive gameplanning, and that's how he would help the Giants become one of the top teams in the NFL. Four of his teams allowed the fewest points in the NFL, and the Giants were in the top three in that category ten times. Nasty, hardhitting, and effective defensive play was his calling card as coach of the New York Football Giants. (They were regularly referred to that way to avoid confusion with the baseball team by the same name. The baseball Giants moved to San Francisco following the 1957 season.)

Owen didn't mind if an opponent drove the field on his defense and had to settle for three-pointers. It was part of Owen's bend-but-don't-break philosophy.

Owen believed that if he could prevent offenses from making big plays and force them to drive the field, they would make mistakes. His goal was to have his defense in a position to take advantage of those mistakes and take the ball away from his opponents.

Owen was one of the first coaches to pay serious attention to defense in practice every day, and his "Umbrella" setup with four defensive backs playing in the secondary became the forerunner of the base 4-3 defense that remains one of the staples of modern defensive play.

Owen laid the foundation for the Giants in his first two years with the team when they were quite ordinary. However, by the 1933 season they had absorbed his lessons and became a consistent championship contender. From 1933 through the 1946 season, the Giants played in eight NFL Championship games.

While they won only two of those games, both of those championship teams were quite legendary. The 1934 Giants won the East Division with an 8-5-0 record, and that allowed them to host the championship game against George Halas's Bears, who had ripped their way through the league with a 13-0 record. The Bears had rocked the Giants 27-7 in Chicago during the regular season, and nobody expected the Giants to reverse that outcome even though they were playing in New York at the Polo Grounds. Nevertheless, Halas knew that whenever his team played the Giants, it was going to feature great defensive play that was all about keeping the Bears out of the end zone and making them settle for field goal attempts.

Throughout the first three quarters of the game that was played in icy conditions at the venerable stadium, the Bears dictated the pace and built a 13-3 lead. But the Giants were not about to surrender. At the start of the fourth quarter, they changed their footwear from ineffective spikes to conventional gym shoes. Giants end Ray Flaherty had suggested to Owen that the players would be more effective in basketball shoes that gripped the surface, so Owen had an assistant retrieve nine pairs of the shoes from nearby Manhattan College.

Suddenly, the Giants came to life at the start of the final quarter as quarterback Ed Danowski threw one touchdown pass and ran for another, while running back Ken Strong had two touchdown runs. By the time the final fifteen minutes had concluded, the Giants had outscored the Bears 27-0 and ended the Bears' eighteen-game winning streak. Halas and his players were flabbergasted. That championship contest would live on in NFL history as "The Sneakers Game."

The Giants would meet the Green Bay Packers in the 1938 title game after winning the East Division with an 8-2-1 record. The Giants were surging, as they went 7-0-1 to finish the regular season after starting with two losses in three games. They had a solid offense led by Danowski and Tuffy Leemans, but the Packers were a more explosive offensive team, with Cecil Isbell passing and Arnie Herber running the ball.

The Giants would outlast Green Bay 23-17, as Owen's defense forced three turnovers to seal the deal for New York.

Owen's conservative nature was an issue in the Giants' other championship game appearances. While he was content to try to establish the run in those games, opponents came up with more innovative offenses and that put the Giants at a disadvantage.

He would come around and later start to use the T-formation that nearly all of his opponents had installed years before, but Owen would never embrace that offensive formation. He preferred to tinker with the defense, and didn't take advantage of the skill that his faster players had.

As the years went along, Owen followed a practice held by many veteran coaches. He trusted his long time players and looked on rookies and other less experienced players with disdain. That caused a rift between him and his younger players, and that showed in the Giants' 41-40-3 record over the final seven years of his tenure in New York.

Eventually, Owen was fired by Wellington Mara after the 1953 season. Owen always thought that football was a series of one-on-one battles, and the team with the stronger and tougher men would win the majority of those battles. He tended to ignore strategy that would take advantage of speed and quickness.

While it was a tough way for his career with the Giants to come to an end, few coaches were ever able to build teams that played as consistently as Owen's Giants. They played with so much ferocity on defense, and that's the legacy that got him elected to the Hall of Fame in 1966.

For the record

Steve Owen
Hall of Fame, 1996
Regular-season record: 151–100–17, .602
Postseason record: 2–8, .200
Two NFL championships

#35

MIKE SHANAHAN

John Elway was desperate after the 1994 season. He had been playing in the NFL since 1983 and had gotten close to winning the Super Bowl three times.

He had been the triggerman for three AFC Championship teams, and each one of those teams had lost in the Super Bowl. Each of those defeats had been more humiliating than the one before, and Elway did not want his career to conclude without a Super Bowl ring.

Many players feel the same way, but are often powerless to do anything about it. Elway may have been the best quarterback of his generation and there were no doubts about his physical gifts.

Elway had spent the majority of his career working with Dan Reeves to bring the Broncos a title, but when that relationship ran its course after the 1992 season, Reeves was sent packing by owner Pat Bowlen at the urging of the quarterback.

The Broncos were ordinary the next two seasons under Wade Phillips, going 9-7 and then 7-9. Phillips was relieved of his coaching duties, and Elway was sure who he wanted to coach the Broncos.

He went to the Super Bowl following that season and sought out Mike Shanahan, who was the offensive coordinator of the San Francisco 49ers. San Francisco was days away from winning the Super Bowl title against the upstart San Diego Chargers, and Elway went to Miami to convince Shanahan to become the next head coach of the Broncos.

Shanahan had been an offensive coordinator with the Broncos, and Elway loved his offensive creativity. That aspect of the Broncos offense had been put asunder by Reeves's conservative nature, and Elway knew in his heart that if he was going to win a Super Bowl in the final years of his career, he needed a great mind like Shanahan's to lead him to it.

Shortly after the Niners annihilated the Chargers, Shanahan became head coach of the Broncos, and Elway could not have been more relieved.

He knew there were no guarantees that the Broncos would get to the Super Bowl and win it, but he knew that Shanahan represented his last and best chance to get there.

Shanahan took the job, the second NFL head coaching position of his career. He had coached the Los Angeles Raiders in 1988 and into the '89 season, but that position fell apart when he started bumping heads with Al Davis. Shanahan's tenure with the Raiders ended four games into his second season with them and it was an ugly divorce that resulted in disdain between the two for twenty years.

By the time he became the Broncos' top gun, he was a fully mature coach who had his own game plan, could communicate it to his players, and excelled at teaching the game.

He laid the groundwork for his coaching tenure in 1995 during an 8-8 season, but the Broncos became an elite team after that. They were 13-3 in 1996 and the top seed in the AFC playoffs, and they were expected to roll through the postseason.

Strangely and shockingly, the Broncos lost a divisional playoff game to the upstart Jacksonville Jaguars, a defeat that left the city of Denver shaking and wondering if the team would ever win a championship.

But Shanahan was not shaken. He knew the talent was there and that the Broncos would continue to contend for the title. In addition to Elway, Shanahan had upgraded the Broncos' offensive line and drafted a sensational running back in Terrell Davis.

Elway had never had a viable running game to support him in the past, but Davis changed that. He was a powerful between-the-tackles runner who had the speed to run away from tacklers once he got to the second level.

Davis rushed for 1,538 yards in '96, and he followed that up with a 1,750-yard season and 15 touchdowns in '97. That ability to run the ball gave the Broncos' offense a dynamic quality that had been missing from other Broncos' teams in the past.

Elway was more than happy to take advantage of the newly found versatility of the running game. At the age of thirty-seven, Elway was still a gifted quarterback with a powerful arm, but he was no longer the swift athlete who could outrun the defense consistently. The presence of Davis meant opponents were forced to defend the run, and not just pay lip service.

So the defeat in the '96 postseason may have been painful for everyone within the organization, but it just steeled Shanahan more for the '97 season. After a 12-4 season, the Broncos were back in the postseason and their first opponent was Jacksonville once again.

There would be no repeat of the previous year's debacle. The Broncos rolled to a 42-17 triumph, and that victory gave them confidence to move forward.

The Broncos followed up with road triumphs over the Chiefs in the divisional playoffs and came up with a huge upset over the Steelers in Pittsburgh that earned them a trip to Super Bowl XXXII against the Green Bay Packers, in San Diego.

Green Bay had won the championship the year before and the combination of head coach Mike Holmgren and Brett Favre appeared to be an unbeatable one. Additionally, NFC teams had won a remarkable twelve straight Super Bowls, and the Packers were huge favorites to win this game as well.

Green Bay had confidently swaggered around San Diego in the days before the game with an edge that bordered on conceit. The Packers came out on fire, as Favre hit Antonio Freeman with an early twenty-two-yard touchdown pass, and many thought the rout was on.

However, it was just the first blow in a heavyweight fight. The Broncos hit back with a big play every time Green Bay made one, and that seemed to shock the Packers. Davis and Elway scored first-half touchdowns to give the Broncos the lead, but the game was tight throughout.

Shanahan had helped his team stand up to what many thought was a superior opponent, and they got the inspiration to win the game when Elway converted a crucial fourth down by taking two big hits and running for a first down late in the third quarter. When his teammates saw him make that play, they were not about to lose.

Davis scored the go-ahead touchdown in a 31-24 victory, and the defense stopped Favre on his final drive when his fourth-down pass to Mark Chmura was batted away.

The Broncos and Elway had their title, and Shanahan was the architect.

The Broncos defended that title the following year by beating the Atlanta Falcons, who were coached by Reeves.

In turn, Elway retired with two consecutive championships.

Shanahan coached the Broncos for ten more seasons and made four more playoff appearances, but the team could not get back to the Super Bowl. Shanahan and the Broncos parted company after the 2008 season, and he was often criticized for never winning another Super Bowl without Elway on his side.

However, it should be noted that Elway never won a Super Bowl without Shanahan.

Shanahan moved on to the Washington Redskins and spent four seasons with them, making the playoffs once. His tenure in Washington never had the even flow and consistency that it did in Denver, and the 2013 season was his last.

Shanahan's discipline, preparation, offensive creativity, knowledge of personnel, and ability to bring about the best from his players allowed him to win back-to-back Super Bowls and earn one of the most respected reputations in the game.

For the record

Mike Shanahan
Regular-season record: 170–138–0, .552
Postseason record: 8–6, .5718
Two Super Bowl victories

#36

GREASY NEALE

Alfred Earle "Greasy" Neale was a part of sports history long before he became head coach of the Philadelphia Eagles in 1941.

As an athlete, he was a major league baseball player in addition to a college football and basketball star. His most noteworthy athletic achievements came as a baseball player for the Cincinnati Reds. Neale played outfield for the Reds from 1916 through 1924, and batted .259 over that span.

While his overall play was average, he played a starring role for the Reds in the 1919 World Series, when he batted .357 with 10 hits in 28 at-bats against the Chicago White Sox. Few remember that Series for anything other than the fact that the heavily favored

White Sox infamously threw the series at the behest of gambler Arnold Rothstein.

That didn't impact Neale, who lashed line drives throughout the series.

But Neale's heart was in football, and he coached college football even as he played in the major leagues. His big break appeared to come when he was hired to coach at West Virginia in 1931, but he struggled to win with the Mountaineers and moved on to Yale in 1934, where he served as the team's backfield coach.

Neale had been known as an innovative coach throughout his twenty-five-year run as a college coach. One of his most important moves was to give defensive linemen an alternative to charging straight ahead and attempting to overpower offensive linemen on every play.

Instead, Neale had his inside linemen loop to the outside before charging into the backfield, with his defensive ends looping to the inside. Neale devised these "stunts" to confuse opposing blockers and give his defensive line a chance to gather momentum before they attempted to stop plays in the backfield.

Owner Lex Thompson hired Neale to coach the Philadelphia Eagles in 1941. Thompson was a Yale alumnus who was quite impressed with Neale's knowledge of the game and his coaching ability.

However, Neale inherited a poor team that had never had a winning season, and he knew he couldn't win with the players he had on his roster. A year after he was hired, the World War II effort took away many of the Eagles players—as it had from other teams throughout the league—and that prevented Neale from making any significant moves with the roster.

However, the team grew steadily stronger, and by the time the war ended, Neale had a team that included quarterback Tommy Thompson, end Pete Pihos, and running backs Steve Van Buren and "Bosh" Pritchard.

Neale was a demanding coach on the practice field who would not tolerate mistakes. He was bold, loud, and intimidating, and he had an amazing ability to pick out the slightest flaw he saw on the practice field, explain it to his players, and correct it immediately.

Unlike most coaches who came across as disciplinarians on the field, he was not afraid to show another side to his personality off the field. He was friendly and gregarious away from the football field, and the same players that he upbraided on the field a few hours earlier genuinely enjoyed spending time with him off of it.

That helped the Eagles become a close-knit team. He led them to their first winning record in 1943, and they never had a losing record throughout the rest of his tenure, which ended in 1950.

Neale helped the Eagles build one of the NFL's most consistent offenses throughout the 1940s. Like many other football coaches, he was shocked and impressed when the Chicago Bears destroyed the Washington Redskins by a 73-0 margin in the 1940 NFL Championship game with their innovative T-formation.

Neale studied Chicago's format and gave the Eagles an improved version. While the Bears had concentrated on running the ball between the tackles, Neale made sure his team also had the option of taking plays to the outside. As he perfected the Eagles' version of the T, he also built a counter formation for his defense.

He knew that nearly all of his competition would be running some version of the T, so building a defense that could stop it was essential to winning. Neale devised a 5-4-2 format, which was quite naturally called the Eagle defense.

Additionally, Neale originated the concept of man-to-man coverage in defending the pass, and then putting as many as nine men on the line in a goalline defense. Teams did not stack the line of scrimmage when opponents were threatening until Neale came up with the concept.

By the 1947 season, the Eagles were functioning at a very high level. They tied the Pittsburgh Steelers with an 8-4 record, good for first in the East Division, and whipped Pittsburgh 21-0 to earn a spot in the NFL Championship game against the Chicago Cardinals.

The Eagles were playing catch-up throughout the game, and when Chicago's Elmer Angsman ran seventy yards for a touchdown in the fourth period, Chicago took a 28-14 lead. The Eagles closed to within seven points when Russ Craft scored on a one-yard run, but they could get no closer.

The Eagles were sharper and even more focused the following year when they rolled to a 9-2-1 record. They faced the Cardinals again in the 1948 season opener, and dropped a 21-14 decision, but they were nearly unbeatable from that point forward.

When the Cardinals came to Philadelphia for an NFL Championship game rematch, the two teams were forced to play in a brutal snowstorm. It was nearly impossible for either team to sustain an offense, but Van Buren scored the only touchdown in the fourth quarter and the Eagles had their first NFL title.

The Eagles were even better in 1949, as they rolled to an 11-1 record. They were clearly the best team in the league, but the NFL did not offer home field advantage to the team with the best record in the league. Since they had hosted the NFL Championship game as the East Division champion against the West Division's Cardinals the previous year, they were forced to play at the West Division champion's home field in 1949.

It was a trip that Neale and his players enjoyed thoroughly. Instead of playing in cold and snowy Philadelphia, the Eagles went to sunny Los Angeles to play the Rams. The Eagles had defeated Los Angeles 38-14 earlier in the year and they treated the game like a vacation. The Rams offered little resistance as Philadelphia won its second consecutive title by a 14-0 margin, thanks to a Pihos touchdown pass from Tommy Thompson and a blocked punt for a score.

The Eagles played the most significant Opening Day game in the history of the NFL at the start of the 1950 season. The NFL had allowed the Cleveland Browns, San Francisco 49ers, Baltimore Colts, and New York Yanks from the All-American Football Conference to join the NFL. The Browns had been the dominant team in that league, and Paul Brown's team met Neale's Eagles in the opener.

Once again, the Eagles had a cavalier attitude towards their opponent from a supposedly inferior league. But head coach Paul Brown had the redoubtable Otto Graham at quarterback and the Browns came into Philadelphia and trounced the Eagles 35-10.

That defeat resounded with the Eagles, who had grown older and less efficient. They fell to 6-6-0 that season, and when Lex Thompson sold the team to a syndicate headed by temperamental James Clark, Neale lost his job security.

Clark barged into the locker room following a late-season defeat at the hands of the Giants and criticized Neale in front of his players. Neale responded back in kind, and he was let go by the Eagles at the end of the season.

Neale's run with the Eagles represented the glory years in Philadelphia. They would win another title in 1960, but they have not won another one since then.

Neale was a sharp and innovative coach who turned the fortunes of the Eagles around in a dramatic fashion.

For the record

> **Greasy Neale**
> Hall of Fame, 1969
> Regular-season record: 63-43-5, .594
> Postseason record: 3-1, .750
> Two NFL championships

#37

JEFF FISHER

Jeff Fisher was slated to play a key role with the 1985 Chicago Bears, perhaps the greatest defensive team in the history of the NFL.

Fisher was a defensive back with Chicago and also a solid punt returner, and he thought through the game like a coach on the field from the time the Bears drafted him in 1981. However, Fisher hurt his ankle and he was placed on Injured Reserve prior to the start of that season, and he had to watch that great defense play from the sidelines.

Fisher had already impressed Bears defensive coordinator Buddy Ryan with his knowledge of the game prior to 1985, but it became obvious to Ryan and others that Fisher's future was on the sidelines.

When Ryan was named head coach of the Philadelphia Eagles prior to the 1986 season, he took Fisher with him as one of his defensive assistants. He became the Eagles' defensive coordinator by 1988, and there was little doubt that he was one of the fastest-rising coaches in the business.

When the Eagles parted company with Ryan after the 1990 season, they interviewed Fisher as one of the top two candidates for the head coaching job. However, in a decision that would prove to be one of the worst in Eagles history, they went with offensive coordinator Rich Kotite instead of Fisher.

Fisher continued to hone his coaching skills with the Los Angeles Rams under John Robinson, and then he became the Houston Oilers' defensive coordinator.

Fisher was itching for a head coaching position, and he finally got his opportunity when the Oilers parted company with veteran head coach Jack Pardee. They turned their miserable 1-9 team over to Fisher, and he was not able to do much as the Oilers finished the season by winning just one of their last six games.

However, Fisher established his coaching style over those final weeks of the 1994 season, and he became one of those rare individuals who could speak honestly to his players without losing them.

Fisher has always been blunt in his assessments, but he has the gift of being able to speak the truth without his players or assistant coaches hating him for telling them exactly where they stood. Many players will say they want someone who will tell them the truth and let them know where they stand, but they get uncomfortable or insecure when they actually hear it.

More than anything, Fisher's players have always worked hard for him and respected him because he doesn't lie to them. Many head coaches speak around the truth, but few will actually look their players in the eye, tell them exactly what they need to do, and then hold the players and themselves accountable to those requirements.

That's exactly how Fisher has done his job, even through his present-day job as coach of the St. Louis Rams, a team that has gone through some bad years. "In a way, it has been easy for me to treat players that way," Fisher said. "I know how I wanted to be treated as a player and I know that the best coaches are dead honest with them. That's what I believe that nearly every player wants and that's how I treat my players."

Fisher's Oilers showed immediate improvement as they went 7-9 and 8-8 in 1995 and '96, but owner Bud Adams left Houston after that year and took his squad to Tennessee in 1997. It was one of the most difficult years in NFL history for any team, because the squad's new headquarters was in Nashville, but the team played its first season in Memphis, some 212 miles away.

In many ways, the newly named Titans played 16 road games in 1997, and that was a big reason why the team went 8-8. They had to do the same thing in '98, and had another .500 season.

However, they finally moved into their new stadium in Nashville in 1999, changed their name from the Oilers to the Titans, and went 13-3.

In most years, that kind of record would earn a team a division title and a likely bye in the first round of the NFL playoffs. However, the Titans finished second in the AFC South to the 14-2 Jacksonville Jaguars and were forced to travel the wild-card route in the playoffs.

The Titans were tested in the first round by the Buffalo Bills, and it seemed that the Bills would walk out of the Adelphia Coliseum with a 16-15 victory when Buffalo placekicker Steve Christie connected on a forty-one-yard field goal with twenty seconds left on the clock.

But the Titans had been well-prepared by Fisher to overcome the desperate straits in which they found themselves. Tight end Frank Wycheck picked up the kickoff and ran a few steps to his right before turning 180 degrees and lateraling the ball back in the direction he came from. The ball landed in the midsection of speedy return specialist Kevin Dyson, who turned upfield with excellent blocking in front of him and ran seventy-five yards for the game-winning touchdown.

That play became known as the "Music City Miracle."

The Titans used that play to spur them on a great postseason run. They defeated the Indianapolis Colts 19-16 in the divisional play-offs before going to Jacksonville to take on the Jaguars. The Titans were supremely confident they would win that game because they had defeated Jacksonville twice in the regular season. Tennessee rolled behind quarterback Steve McNair, running back Eddie George, and a hard-nosed defense and earned the AFC title with a 33-14 victory.

The Titans faced the St. Louis Rams in the Super Bowl, where they fell behind Dick Vermeil's explosive team 16-0 before mounting a dramatic comeback that allowed them to tie the score at 16-16. The Rams rebounded to take the lead, but the Titans had a chance to score the tying touchdown. On the game's final play, McNair hit Dyson with a short pass and the receiver appeared to be going into the end zone for the tying touchdown. However, St. Louis line-backer Mike Jones brought Dyson down at the one-yard line and the Titans absorbed a crushing defeat.

Fisher has never gotten back to the Super Bowl. His Tennessee teams made four more playoff appearances, but they never had quite enough offensive balance or consistent quarterback play to get to the top of the football world.

Fisher eventually resigned following the 2010 season, and took a year off before resurfacing with the Rams. While he has not brought the Rams back to glory, they are respected as a hard-nosed and honest team that plays nasty and aggressive defense.

Fisher has been a head coach for twenty years, and his honest, straight-forward approach has made him one of the most successful and popular head coaches through the 2014 season.

For the record

Jeff Fisher
Regular-season record: 162–147–1, .524
Postseason record: 5–6, .455

#38

BUDDY PARKER

It is so common today that most football fans can't remember a time when teams didn't run a fast-paced, no-huddle offense at the end of the half or at the conclusion of the game when it was trying to catch up and valuable seconds were draining off the clock.

However, the two-minute offense is not just a part of football the way that gravity is a part of daily existence. It was not born with the game.

It was, in part, an invention of the fertile mind of Raymond "Buddy" Parker. However, Parker did not come to invent the two-minute offense by himself. In fact, he never would have come by it if it had not been for the prowess of Bobby Layne, Parker's quarterback in Detroit.

Not only was Layne way ahead of his time, but he also was a hard-living man who loved to chase women and drink off the football field, and he didn't like to be reined in by football coaches or game plans.

When Layne walked on to the football field, he wanted to call the plays that best suited him and his teammates. After all, he was the one on the field, and it was his body and career that were on the line. He didn't see any reason to comply with a coach's suggestion.

Except that he understood that he was the employee and the coach was the boss, and most of the time he worked under the parameters of the offense, even if he didn't like it. Most of the time. Not all of the time.

Parker also had an ego similar to Layne's, and the two butted heads often. He thought of Layne as a rule breaker who wanted to do what he saw fit on the football field, and that did not make Parker happy.

However, Parker also saw that Layne was one of the most accomplished quarterbacks in the game and he was perhaps the best leader at his position in the NFL. So while they didn't always agree during Parker's tenure as head coach of the Detroit Lions between 1951 and 1956, they also worked well together and forged consistent success with the Lions.

Parker led the Lions to three straight NFL Championship games between 1952 and 1954, and they won two of those games. He also was the first coach to use a "two-minute offense" in the final stages of either half. Layne would rush his team to the line of scrimmage, and either run the play that was called or audible out of it in a matter of seconds.

The quarterback did this with Parker's approval and urging. It was very successful, as the Lions won twenty-eight of thirty-six regular-season games in those seasons.

Parker was a colorful coach from Texas, who got his first chance as a head coach in the NFL with the Chicago Cardinals. He was initially one of Jimmy Conzelman's trusted assistant coaches and he basically handled much of the offensive coaching.

When Conzelman left after the 1948 season, Parker and Phil Handler were named co-coaches of the team, but the team booted Handler upstairs prior to midseason and let Parker handle the head coaching duties. He led the Cardinals to a 4-1-1 record in the second half, which gave them a 6-5-1 record for the season.

But instead of preparing for his first full season as the team's lone coach, Parker decided to quit the Cardinals. He could not stomach the front office's meddling ways, and he figured that if he could not coach the team his way without interference, it wasn't a job he wanted.

Parker immediately went to the Lions as an assistant to "Bo" McMillin, and that turned out to be a fateful move. The Lions players liked Parker and they despised McMillin, and he was fired at the end of the 1950 season.

Layne, Doak Walker, and Cloyce Box, the three stars of the Lions, were thrilled by the move because they saw Parker as a coach who could help them win. Mainly, they liked him because he was not McMillin.

Parker did not have a lot of rules for his players off the field. He did not give them a curfew, and that suited Layne just fine. He also turned over much of the defense to his trusted friend Buster Ramsey, and Ramsey was able to build a unit that ranked in the league's top three defenses four times during his tenure.

That allowed Parker to spend much of his time building an explosive offensive team. While Layne would often do as he pleased on the field, Parker was able to offer suggestions to the quarterback that turned out to be successful. That's because Parker spent much of his time studying film of the opposition, and he could find weaknesses that weren't so obvious to the other coaches.

Layne knew that Parker was gifted in this area, particularly when the coach would make adjustments at halftime. Those adjustments were not based on feel or gut instincts that were the hallmark of Layne's career, but on the study and hard work that Parker had done by watching film.

Parker was one of the most successful coaches of his era while he was with the Lions, but he abruptly quit the team prior to the start of the 1957 season. At the time he stepped down, he claimed the team had looked awful in training camp and was not capable of winning consistently.

Some reporters claimed that that wasn't the real reason, but rather that Parker had been negotiating a new contract with the Lions, and when the process got bogged down and he didn't get the deal he wanted, he decided he was not going to do any more talking.

Weeks later, Parker was hired as head coach of the Pittsburgh Steelers. At the time, Pittsburgh was a moribund team that lacked star players and endured losing season after losing season.

Parker was able to help the Steelers play much more respectable football. He coached the Steelers from 1957 through 1964, and he led them to five seasons (out of the eight that he was there) in which they were .500 or better.

He was quirky and superstitious, and he liked to have a controlling hand on personnel. This proved to be his undoing. During training camp prior to the 1965 season, he tried to trade Chuck Hinton and Ben McGee to the Philadelphia Eagles. Hinton and McGee were two of the team's top defensive linemen, and when owner Art Rooney heard he wanted to do this and get Philadelphia backup quarterback King Hill, he rejected the deal.

Parker quit in a huff and never coached in the NFL again. However, he basically invented the two-minute drill and honed his game-planning by studying film as it had rarely been done before.

That gave Parker a legacy that made him one of the top coaches of his era.

For the record

Buddy Parker
Regular-season record: 104–75–9, .581
Postseason record: 3–1, .750
Two NFL championships

#39

DICK VERMEIL

Dick Vermeil shed more tears in his coaching career than a room full of brides do.

He shed tears of sadness, tears of happiness, and tears of joy. Vermeil was a brilliant coach who set trends and precedents throughout his career, and celebrated every one of them.

Vermeil was smart, thoughtful, and organized to begin with, and he began to make a name for himself as an assistant coach on John Ralston's Stanford staff in the 1960s. George Allen, who was head coach of the Los Angeles Rams at the time, took notice of Vermeil, and hired him to become the first special teams coach in NFL history.

It was a move that all pro teams quickly copied, because Vermeil did the job so well that it was quite clear that getting the advantage on special teams could make a huge difference. Vermeil became a trusted assistant coach in both the NFL and college, and that allowed him to earn his first head-coaching position when he was hired at UCLA in 1974.

Vermeil turned the Bruins into winners and he became one of the most sought-after NFL head coaching prospects when he led UCLA to a Rose Bowl upset over Ohio State.

The Philadelphia Eagles organization was the most persistent suitor and eventually hired Vermeil prior to the 1976 season.

Many people thought Vermeil had lost his senses because the Eagles were a brutal team that had not had a winning record in nine seasons. The Eagles were loaded with out-of-shape players, and drug use was rampant.

Vermeil got rid of those players and turned over the roster. He didn't care about a player's previous accomplishments. He just wanted hard-nosed players who had a single-minded determination to play winning football.

It wasn't enough for Vermeil to find the players. He had to put everything he had into the job, and that often meant staying in the office overnight or working as many as twenty hours per day.

His efforts began to pay off in his third year with the team when the Eagles finished with a 9-7 record. Players like Ron Jaworski, Wilbert Montgomery, Herman Edwards, and Carl Hairston helped get the Eagles going, and they gave their emotional coach everything they had.

The 1979 season saw the Eagles earn a playoff spot with an 11-5 record. They defeated the Chicago Bears 27-17 in the wild-card game, but they dropped their divisional playoff matchup to the Tampa Bay Buccaneers.

That game stayed with Vermeil and the Eagles through the off-season and it was their motivation in 1980. The Eagles became a legitimate Super Bowl contender, winning the NFC East with a

12-4 record, because they held a tiebreaker edge over Tom Landry and his Dallas Cowboys.

The Eagles earned the right to host the NFC Championship game when they defeated the overmatched Minnesota Vikings 31-16.

The Cowboys had upset the Atlanta Falcons and they came to Philadelphia with a mind to do the same thing to the Eagles. Landry and the Cowboys were football royalty, and many assumed their pedigree would get them over the top in this crucial game.

But the Eagles proved nastier, tougher, and meaner, as they came through with a 20-7 triumph behind the spectacular running of Montgomery, who scored the opening touchdown of the game on a forty-two-yard run and finished with 194 yards.

The Eagles went to the Super Bowl for the first time and they faced the wild-card Oakland Raiders, who had defeated the Houston Oilers, Cleveland Browns, and San Diego Chargers to become the first wild-card team to get to the Super Bowl.

The Eagles seemed to be the bigger, stronger, and more physical team, but the Raiders were more opportunistic and were savvy. Linebacker Rod Martin intercepted three of Jaworski's passes, and quarterback Jim Plunkett threw three touchdown passes as the Raiders came away with a shockingly easy 27-10 triumph.

That loss stayed with Vermeil for years, and his Eagles started to backslide. They made the playoffs the following year, but were eliminated by the New York Giants in the wild-card game, and they fell badly the following year.

Vermeil quit after that season, as he had gotten so emotional that he had a difficult time adjusting to family life. "I'm my own worst enemy," Vermeil said upon leaving the Eagles. "I am far too intense and far too emotional."

Vermeil was burned-out when he left the Eagles, and that term became part of the national lexicon shortly thereafter.

Still, few expected Vermeil to stay away from coaching for more than two years. Yet, that's just what he did. He became a college football analyst and stayed away from the NFL for fourteen years. It seemed he would remain in the TV booth and grow wine grapes in Napa indefinitely.

However, he still had a desire to get back to coaching, and he took a job coaching the Rams in 1997. It appeared Vermeil had little left, as the Rams had two consecutive losing seasons.

However, Vermeil knew his team was loaded with talent as it prepared for the 1999 season. The Rams took what appeared to be a devastating blow when starting quarterback Trent Green suffered a season-ending knee injury in the preseason, but backup Kurt Warner was there to answer the bell.

Warner, a former Arena Football League quarterback, turned out to be one of the most accurate passers in NFL history.

He led "The Greatest Show on Turf" to a first-place finish in the NFC West, and the Rams rolled through the playoffs and earned a spot in Super Bowl XXXIV against the Tennessee Titans. With the scored tied 16-16 late in the fourth quarter, Warner hit wide receiver Isaac Bruce with a seventy-three-yard touchdown pass to give the Rams a 23-16 lead.

The desperate Titans fought back, but Rams linebacker Mike Jones tackled Tennessee wide receiver Kevin Dyson on the St. Louis one-yard line on the game's final play.

The Rams and Vermeil had their Super Bowl title, and the tears flowed for Vermeil. He hugged and kissed his family members, he hugged and kissed his players, and he hugged and kissed his coaches.

He retired again from coaching, but this time he came back in just two years to lead the Kansas City Chiefs in 2001.

He helped turn the Chiefs into a winning team, but they never had the playoff glory that either of his other teams had.

Vermeil retired again following the 2005 season.

His last team went 10-6, and the emotional coach left on his own terms. He was beloved by many of his players from all three teams, and his legacy of hard work, dedication, and long hours remains intact.

For the record

Dick Vermeil
Regular-season record: 120-109-0, .524
Postseason record: 6-5, .545
One Super Bowl victory

#40

GEORGE ALLEN

It's a fairly common story to hear that modern NFL coaches spend twelve, fourteen, or sixteen hours a day during the season working on game plans and preparing to compete against an opponent.

George Allen was the first of these single-minded coaches who put so much of his time into preparing for a game. He did this because he was obsessed with not losing.

The obsession was not with winning. When Allen's team won games, he would jump for joy, lead his teams in cheers, and celebrate with his beloved vanilla ice cream. But when it was over, he would begin the process anew.

However, if his team lost, Allen was crestfallen and deeply disturbed. "Every time you win, you are reborn," Allen said. "But when you lose, you die a little."

Allen came into his own when he was hired by George Halas to serve as a scout in the 1958 season. Specifically, Halas wanted Allen to scout the Los Angeles Rams. Allen gave Halas and his players a report that was so thorough and cogent that it gave the team a succinct game plan to follow.

Halas, a curmudgeon who was never easily impressed, realized that Allen was one of the sharpest men he had ever worked with and he hired him to be an assistant coach with the Bears. In addition to that job, Halas also asked Allen to do all the preparation work for the Bears' drafts, and run those as well.

During the time that Allen was in charge of the Bears' college player procurement, they drafted Mike Ditka, Dick Butkus, and Gale Sayers. Those were not only Hall of Fame players with dominant ability, but also three of the greatest players who have ever played the game.

Halas was now thoroughly impressed, and he made Allen his defensive coordinator in 1963, a move that his players applauded. Allen installed a defensive scheme that was based heavily on the zone blitz, and the results were remarkable.

The Bears finished 11-1-2 that season and won the NFL's West Division. They had a mundane offense that featured Bill Wade at quarterback and running backs Joe Marconi and Ronnie Bull. Neither Marconi nor Bull topped the 500-yard mark, while Wade threw for 2,301 yards and had a 15-12 touchdown-interception ratio. Ditka was the star of the offense, as he caught 59 passes for 794 yards and eight touchdowns.

However, the defense was simply remarkable, and it allowed just 144 points in fourteen games. Overpowering players like Doug Atkins, Ed O'Bradovich, J. C. Caroline, Rosey Taylor, Richie

Petitbon, and Davey "The Weasel" Whitsell pounded opponents and regularly took away the ball from them.

The Bears beat the New York Giants 14-10 in the 1963 NFL Championship game at Soldier Field, and that would be the last title the team would win under Halas.

Shortly after that, Halas told Allen he would become head coach of the Bears after he retired. However, Halas was still coaching the Bears through the 1965 season, and he did not offer any indications that he would be leaving in the foreseeable future.

As a result, Allen left the Bears to become head coach of the Rams. Subsequently, Halas grew angry that Allen would not remain with the Bears and patiently continue to wait. Halas held a grudge against Allen from that point on, a grudge that he never got over.

Allen's meticulous ways worked wonders with the Rams. He took over a team that had been 4-10 in 1965, and immediately started making trades and personnel moves. Allen did not think the Rams had the kind of personnel that could win in the NFL, and he was determined to make sure they improved quickly. If that meant trading draft picks for veteran players, he was more than willing to do just that.

The Rams became a winning team in 1966 with an 8-6-0 record, but that was just the beginning. They finished 11-1-2 in 1967, and they closed the regular season with seven straight wins. The final two wins of the season came against Vince Lombardi's Green Bay Packers and Don Shula's Baltimore Colts.

Wins over those two brilliant coaches raised Allen's status in a powerful way, and the Rams went into the postseason with full momentum. Some thought the Rams would be able to repeat their earlier win over the Packers, but when they were forced to go to Lambeau Field and play Lombardi's team in its preferred element, the Rams fell short by a 28-7 margin.

Still, Allen had come a long way in a short period of time because his team had tremendous pass rushing abilities, thanks to its "Fearsome Foursome" that included "Deacon" Jones, Merlin Olsen, Roger Brown, and Lamar Lundy. The Rams' offense was quite conservative, but the defense was reckless and exciting.

The Rams continued to be one of the better regular-season teams over the subsequent three years, but only made the playoffs once, and they lost that game to the Minnesota Vikings.

Allen's quirky style and failure to build an exciting offense angered team owner Dan Reeves, and the 1970 season became Allen's last with the Rams.

The Washington Redskins wasted no time in bringing Allen aboard. They had also been an ordinary team prior to Allen's arrival and had finished 6-8-0 in 1970 with the nondescript Bill Austin at head coach.

Allen immediately started making the same kind of personnel moves with the Redskins that he had with the Rams, as he had an eye towards immediate improvement and was not concerned about anything but the present and the immediate future.

He traded rookies and draft picks for solid veterans, and the Redskins suddenly became competitive. They finished 9-4-1 in 1971, and he sang, danced, and whooped it up when the Redskins won. When reporters asked him what his team would do in the future without all their first-round draft picks since he traded them every year, he didn't hesitate. "The future is now," he declared.

Allen brought his team to the precipice of a championship in 1972. After they finished first in the NFC East Division with an 11-3-0 record, Allen's team won its first playoff game when the Redskins defeated the Packers 16-3.

That relieved a great deal of pressure for Allen, and he got his team prepared as it had never been the following week in the NFC

Championship game against the archrival Dallas Cowboys. The Redskins dominated, with Billy "The Kid" Kilmer throwing the ball and Larry Brown running it, and they pounded Tom Landry's team 26-3.

The victory was so impressive that the Redskins were slight favorites to defeat the Miami Dolphins in Super Bowl VII—even though the Dolphins were undefeated. Miami kept its perfect season intact and won the game by a 14-7 margin.

The Redskins would never get back to the Super Bowl under Allen, and they would never win another playoff game. His teams played consistently in the regular season, but Allen's simplistic offense was fairly easy for opponents to figure out in the postseason, and he never adjusted. Allen left the Redskins when his contract concluded after the 1977 season.

Allen was particularly demanding and difficult to work with, and few teams considered hiring him at that point. However, the Rams once again came calling under new owner Carroll Rosenbloom. Yet Allen did not even make it through the preseason and he was fired after two exhibition games because he was simply too overbearing.

He coached years later in the United States Football League with some success, but he never made it back to the NFL. At one point he tried to smooth things over with Halas, but his old boss refused his attempts at a rapprochement.

Still, Allen had a huge imprint on the NFL. He became the first coach to devote the majority of his hours to looking at film and diagnosing his opponents' weaknesses. He excelled at picking them out and installing the right game plan to take advantage of them.

While he later came to eschew the draft, his ability to find Hall of Famers like Ditka, Butkus, and Sayers is unparalleled. Allen's 2002 induction into the Hall of Fame was most deserved.

For the record

> **George Allen**
> Hall of Fame, 2002
> Regular-season record: 116-47-5, .712
> Postseason record: 2-7, .222
> One conference championship

#41

BRIAN BILLICK

If you took the 2000 Baltimore Ravens and put them in a tournament with the best teams that ever played the game, they would be the team that nobody wanted to play.

The Ravens wouldn't win that tournament because they had a quarterback in Trent Dilfer who lacked all the characteristics needed to be dynamic, but they would have punished any team that they played.

Simply put, the Ravens had one of the greatest defenses the game has ever seen, one that might be bettered by the 1985 Bears and the Steelers of the 1970s, and few others. The defense was, without a doubt, their bread and butter.

That's the irony of Brian Billick's coaching career. When he was hired by the Ravens prior to the 1999 season, he got the job because he was one of the brightest offensive minds the game has ever seen. He was the offensive coordinator for Dennis Green and his explosive Minnesota Vikings teams in the late 1990s, and he helped take a team that seemingly had a different quarterback every season and turn it into one of the greatest offensive juggernauts in NFL history.

Under Billick, the 1998 season was a remarkable one for the Vikings. They went 15-1 during the season and scored an NFL record 556 points. Billick had an offense that included Randall Cunningham at quarterback, wide receivers Randy Moss and Cris Carter, and explosive Robert Smith at running back, and it was a virtual track meet every week.

The Vikings toyed with most opponents and they outscored opponents by 16 points per game. This may have been one of the best teams the game has ever seen, but they didn't get to the Super Bowl. They lost the NFC Championship game at home to the Atlanta Falcons in one of the most shocking upsets in the last twenty years.

But the pain for Billick was only temporary, as the Baltimore Ravens came calling and wanted him to take over their non-descript team. The Ravens were just 6-10 that season, and owner Art Modell knew he had to do something to help his team start to jell.

The Ravens were 8-8 in 1999, but Billick found a spark late in the season. The Ravens were 4-7 and looking quite miserable after dropping a 30-23 decision at home to the Jacksonville Jaguars. However, they won their next four games in impressive fashion, including a 31-24 win in Week 14 at Pittsburgh.

That game helped the Ravens gain confidence, and they were an eye-opening and marauding bunch in the 2000 season.

They weren't doing much with their offense, but they had a bone-jarring defense led by Ray Lewis, Rod Woodson, Peter Boulware, and Jamie Sharper that just shut opponents down.

Still, the Ravens were having problems early in the year, as they were getting nowhere with Tony Banks at quarterback. Baltimore had a 5-3 record at midseason after dropping a 14-6 home decision to the Tennessee Titans. That matchup marked the fourth straight game that the Ravens had not scored a touchdown.

Billick had seen more than enough, and he sat Banks on the bench and made Dilfer his starting quarterback. Dilfer had endured many difficult seasons with the Tampa Bay Bucs before coming to the Ravens and he had little on his resume that would indicate he could do anything but lose games in the NFL, but Billick had a feeling he could steady the team and help it win.

"I never expected any miracles with Trent at quarterback, but I didn't think we needed anything like that," Billick said. "I just wanted him to take advantage of what the defense gave him and not turn the ball over. If he could do that, I thought our defense would get the job done."

The Ravens' streak of touchdown-free games continued the following week when they dropped a 9-6 decision to the Steelers at home, but they turned things around in Week 10 when they drummed the Bengals 27-7. The Ravens did not lose again during the regular season, and they made the playoffs as a wild-card team.

They put on an impressive show in beating the Broncos 21-3 in their first playoff game, but they didn't appear to have much of a chance against the Titans on the road in the divisional playoffs. The presence of Steve McNair and Eddie George gave the Titans a big edge on offense, and there was only so much the Ravens could do.

Nobody explained that to Lewis, who pounded George on every occasion. He wrestled the ball away from the running back just past the midway point of the fourth quarter and took it fifty yards for a touchdown that clinched a 24-10 decision.

Baltimore then went across the country and punched Jon Gruden's Oakland Raiders in the mouth for sixty minutes, earning a trip to the Super Bowl with a 16-3 victory.

The Ravens had turned into a defensive juggernaut by that time, and they were overflowing with confidence when they met the New York Giants in Tampa. New York had an impressive offense led by quarterback Kerry Collins, but it was a brutal defeat for New York.

By the time Collins came off the field following the 34-7 defeat, his face was ashen. He tried to mouth postgame answers to the media, but his body was bruised and his psyche was shattered.

"That's how we play football," Lewis said after the game. "We are going to hit you and we are going to hurt you. The Giants were the best team in the NFC, and they found out today what Ravens football was all about. Punishment. Pain. Non-stop."

In many ways, that championship was a moment of brilliance for Billick. However, the irony of having a spectacular defense was not lost on him.

"The reason I became a football coach was to develop a game plan and give the offense a chance to score every time it had the ball," Billick explained. "It worked quite well with Minnesota, but it never came together in Baltimore."

"Don't get me wrong, because we had a spectacular championship team that was at its best when it mattered most. We shattered people and played overwhelming defense. I couldn't have been prouder."

But it was clear that Billick wanted to have the same kind of offensive success with the Ravens that he had in Minnesota. It never happened.

He had several more good teams in Baltimore and went to the playoffs three more times, but none of his teams were able to recapture the magic of the 2000 Ravens.

Billick never developed the quarterback or the offense he wanted in Baltimore, and the 2007 season was his last with the team. He has since become a color analyst for FOX Sports on the network's NFL broadcasts. While it may have been a frustrating run taken as a whole, Billick had one of the most imposing and intimidating teams of the Super Bowl era, and it helped him earn a spot as one of the top fifty coaches of all time.

For the record

Brian Billick
Regular-season record: 80–64–0, .566
Postseason record: 5–3, .600
One Super Bowl victory

#42

SEAN PAYTON

Sean Payton helped usher in the modern era of the NFL that emphasizes big plays through the pass at the expense of nearly every other aspect of the game. While he won a Super Bowl with the New Orleans Saints in his fourth season as head coach of the team—and that was clearly a brilliant achievement—his devotion to the passing game may be his ultimate legacy as an NFL head coach.

Payton was an Arena Football League quarterback before he got a chance to play in the NFL as a member of the Chicago Bears' replacement team during the player strike of 1987. But once the NFL players returned to action, Payton's playing career was over and he began his coaching career shortly thereafter.

He had college coaching experience at San Diego State (working with Marshall Faulk), Indiana State, Miami of Ohio, and Illinois before he was selected by Ray Rhodes to coach quarterbacks in Philadelphia in 1997. Jim Fassel eventually went after Payton and he became the Giants' offensive coordinator in 2000. However, Fassel took Payton's play-calling responsibilities away from him in 2002, so Payton eventually joined Bill Parcells with the Dallas Cowboys.

Payton was thought of as an up-and-comer prior to his association with Parcells, but he became one of the most desirable coaching candidates during his time in Dallas. He was a coaching finalist in Green Bay and New Orleans in 2006, and while the Packers settled on Mike McCarthy, he was given a chance to turn the Saints around.

The 2006 season was a bit of a miracle for the organization and the New Orleans region, as both were trying to come back from the raging Hurricane Katrina that had torn apart the city a year earlier.

The Saints won their first two games on the road that season, and came home to play their home opener at the Superdome. The Saints' home crowd had always been loud and raucous, but the fans brought it to a new level against the archrival Atlanta Falcons and the Saints recorded a 23-3 victory.

It was a win that let the NFL know that these were not the same old Saints, and that the combination of Payton and free-agent quarterback Drew Brees would take the organization to a new level. Brees had been a solid and resourceful quarterback during his previous five years with the San Diego Chargers, but Payton saw a quarterback who had the talent to play at a superstar level.

That's one of the reasons that Brees chose to continue his career in New Orleans. Payton told the quarterback that he would build his offense around Brees, include all the plays that he had excelled at with the Chargers, and then add more that would help him become even better. That was all Brees needed to hear in order to join forces with the Saints.

New Orleans would go on to win the division title in 2006, and Brees would go on to throw for 4,418 yards with a 26-11 touchdown-interception ratio.

Prior to Payton's arrival, the Saints had won one postseason game in their history. Payton helped change the organization's image, as the Saints earned a bye into the divisional playoffs, where they defeated the Philadelphia Eagles 27-24 and moved on to the NFC Championship game against the Chicago Bears.

Chicago's defense was led by middle linebacker Brian Urlacher, and it held Brees's offense in check until the Saints scored in the final minute of the first half. While New Orleans had momentum playing on the road, it trailed 16-7 at halftime. The Saints threw a further scare in Chicago when Brees connected with speedy Reggie Bush on an eighty-eight-yard catch and run for a score, but the Bears' defense reasserted itself and Chicago advanced to the Super Bowl with a 39-14 victory.

Payton continued to refine his offense and he attempted to build a tough and opportunistic defense. The Saints had a pair of ordinary seasons in 2007 and '08 in which they failed to make the playoffs, but they found their stride in '09 when they played consistently explosive football and dominated the NFC South Division with a 13-3 record.

They went into the playoffs that season as the top seed and they overwhelmed the Arizona Cardinals 45-14, as Brees threw three touchdown passes and Bush returned a punt for a touchdown. That victory gave them home field advantage in the NFC Championship, and Saints fans were delirious at the thought of their team going to the Super Bowl if they could beat Brett Favre and the Minnesota Vikings.

The Vikings tied the score late in regulation and had a chance to win it when they had the ball in New Orleans territory in the closing seconds, but instead of settling for a field goal attempt, Favre tried to throw the ball late and across the middle and his pass was picked off by Tracy Porter to send the game into overtime.

Garrett Hartley connected on a forty-yard field goal to send Payton and the Saints into the Super Bowl against Peyton Manning and the Indianapolis Colts.

It was widely expected that Manning would end the Saints' dreams in a painful manner and the great quarterback would lead his team to its second Super Bowl title. However, Payton had other plans, and he put them boldly into action at the start of the second half.

The Saints trailed 10-6 and were kicking off to start the final thirty minutes. Payton did not want Manning to lead the Colts on a long drive and increase the deficit, so he ordered kicker Thomas Morstead to attempt an onside kick. The Saints recovered the ball and took the lead when Brees hit Pierre Thomas with a 16-yard touchdown pass to give the Saints a 13-10 lead.

That shocking onside kick, recovery, and subsequent touchdown spurred the Saints to a 31-17 victory and gave them the only Super Bowl championship in their history.

While the Saints have had a rather inconsistent defense throughout Payton's run in New Orleans, their offense has regularly been among the best in the league. That unit was never better than in the 2011 season, when the Saints went 13-3 and scored 547 points.

Brees threw for 5,476 yards, completed 71.2 percent of his passes, and had a remarkable 46-14 touchdown-interception ratio. While many expected the Saints to reach the NFC Championship game in an epic confrontation with the equally prolific Green Bay Packers, they were stopped by the 49ers 36-32 in a heart-stopping game in the divisional playoffs.

The Saints thought that another Super Bowl season was at hand after that, but defensive coordinator Gregg Williams was brought down in the offseason by the "Bountygate" scandal, in which Williams rewarded players for laying big hits and injuring opposing star players.

Payton's reputation was also damaged in the fallout from the scandal, as he was suspended for the 2012 season. It was a painful blow for Payton and the Saints, but they came back strong in 2013 with an 11–5 record and a 26–24 victory over the Eagles in the wild-card round. While they were stopped by Seattle in the divisional playoffs, it was an important rebound season for Payton.

He has shown his ability to build one of the most prolific offenses in NFL history, and his teams have been able to rebound from poor defensive seasons quite well. Payton has one of the top offensive minds in the game, and he has shown that his teams almost always have a chance to come back and win any game.

For the record

Sean Payton
Regular-season record: 80–48–0, .625
Postseason record: 6–4, .600
One Super Bowl victory

#43

JOHN HARBAUGH

It would take a lot for any of the modern-day NFL coaches to stay in the business and lead their teams for as long as Tom Landry, Don Shula, or Chuck Noll headed their teams during their Hall of Fame coaching careers.

However, if there's one coach who has shown the consistency in his approach, demeanor, game-planning, and player relations, it's John Harbaugh. He has led the Baltimore Ravens to the postseason in six of his first seven seasons, and his teams have always won at least one playoff game in each of those appearances.

Harbaugh and the Ravens won a Super Bowl following the 2012 season, when his team earned a victory in Super Bowl XLVII over the San Francisco 49ers, a team that was coached by his brother Jim Harbaugh.

John Harbaugh earned his chance to become a head coach in the NFL by climbing the ranks as a college assistant coach and then getting called up to the professional ranks. Harbaugh established a reputation as a coach who understood the details needed to excel at each position, and a talent for building game-changing special teams.

Once word of his work at Morehead State, the University of Cincinnati, and Indiana got out, he got a call from Philadelphia Eagles head coach Ray Rhodes. Philadelphia had endured misery with their special-teams play in 1997, and Rhodes needed a strong, smart, and tough special teams coach who could turn that situation around quickly.

Harbaugh did just that, but the Eagles played awful football in 1998 and Rhodes was fired. However, new coach Andy Reid was impressed by Harbaugh and kept him on the staff. The Eagles' special teams ranked among the best in the league each year. Harbaugh would eventually get moved up the Eagles coaching ladder to defensive backs coach, and Reid knew that Harbaugh would most likely be leaving Philadelphia because he deserved a chance to become a head coach.

The Ravens came calling in 2008, and while Harbaugh did not have much of a reputation for building excellence on the offensive side of the ball, the Ravens were convinced Harbaugh was the right man for the job because of his thoroughness and his ability to remain on even keel even when circumstances called for panic.

The Ravens had a powerful defense at the time, and they were led by stars like linebacker Ray Lewis and safety Ed Reed. However, the offense was rather inconsistent and the team's quarterback play was below average.

That changed during Harbaugh's first year as head coach when the Ravens drafted strong-armed Joe Flacco out of the University of Delaware. While Flacco had the kind of physical tools to make all the throws needed in the NFL, he had not played against upper-level competition with the Blue Hens and he would need time and tutoring to develop into an elite professional quarterback.

Harbaugh understood this from the start, and he never stopped teaching Flacco or believing in him. As a result, the quarterback and the coach became partners in the NFL, and their success was tied to each other.

The Ravens had a very solid season in 2008, recording an 11-5 mark and earning a spot in the playoffs as a wild-card team. The Ravens were 6-4 through their first ten games, but they rolled to a 5-1 finish and were one of the hottest teams in the league at the start of the postseason.

They won postseason road games at Miami and Tennessee before dropping a hard-fought 23-14 decision to the Pittsburgh Steelers in the AFC Championship game.

The Ravens garnered respect with their showing that season, but nobody thought that the Harbaugh-Flacco combination would become a dominant one. The Ravens struggled with their consistency in 2009 and were just 9-7, but that was good enough to earn a postseason appearance.

Nobody expected them to survive their wild-card game against the Patriots, but they went into Foxboro and ran Bill Belichick's team out of its own stadium as they recorded a 33-14 blowout. The Ravens lost the following week at Indianapolis, but Harbaugh had impressed NFL observers with the way he was able to get his team prepared and keep them from getting intimidated against a high-powered opponent like the Patriots.

Harbaugh did an excellent job of establishing firm control of his veteran team, while getting players like Lewis and Reed to buy into his leadership. Harbaugh would never have had an opportunity to become an upper-echelon coach if he had come in with a "my way or the highway" kind of demeanor, but he couldn't give his players the same kind of loose rein that former Baltimore coach Brian Billick had given his team.

It was a delicate balancing act that Harbaugh had to endeavor, and he pulled it off brilliantly.

The Ravens had tremendous confidence as Harbaugh prepared for his third season in 2010, and they continued to play consistently with a 12-4 record. After they rolled to a one-sided 30-7 wild-card victory at Kansas City, their season once again came to an end at the hands of the Pittsburgh Steelers.

The Ravens continued to climb the ladder in 2011, as they won the AFC North title and rolled over the Houston Texans in the divisional playoffs before meeting the Patriots on the road in the AFC Championship game.

Unfortunately for the Ravens, they missed a chance to send the game into overtime when placekicker Billy Cundiff missed a short field goal late in the fourth quarter, and that allowed the Patriots to hold on for a 23-20 victory.

Harbaugh's team came to training camp with a new determination in 2012, and they rolled to a 9-2 start. However, unlike previous Ravens teams, they struggled down the stretch and lost four of their last five regular-season games.

Nobody expected them to do much in the postseason, but the Ravens overpowered the Colts before beating Denver and New England on the road to go to the Super Bowl.

The matchup with the 49ers presented a remarkable brother vs. brother confrontation between the Harbaugh coaches.

The contrast between the two brothers was vital, as John seemed steadier and more mature, while Jim was more emotional and perhaps a touch more creative.

John's Ravens built a big lead and held on to earn a 34-31 victory. Flacco had been brilliant for the Ravens, completing 22-of-33 passes for 287 yards with three touchdowns and no interceptions. Flacco had absorbed much criticism throughout his career, but

Harbaugh had always maintained faith in his quarterback. He was rewarded for that faith with a Super Bowl triumph.

The Super Bowl earned Harbaugh elite status, and his team has been able to win more playoff games on the road than any other team in the Super Bowl era.

Harbaugh's steady demeanor has been one of the key factors for the Ravens, and that's why he has a chance to go on a long run and perhaps join Landry, Shula, and Noll as an institution among head coaches.

For the record

John Harbaugh
Regular-season record: 72-40-0, .643
Postseason record: 10-5, .667
One Super Bowl victory

#44

MIKE DITKA

I t all began with a handwritten letter.

Mike Ditka had been one of the great tight ends in the history of the NFL, and he had been a key player for the Chicago Bears when they won their last NFL championship in 1963 under George Halas.

Ditka not only helped carry the Bears offense on his broad shoulders, but he also helped redefine the tight end position with his big-play ability.

It didn't end well in Chicago, though, as Ditka grew annoyed by Papa Bear's penurious ways. He was traded to Philadelphia in 1968—"the worst year of my life"—before he finished his career with the Dallas Cowboys. He was on Tom Landry's 1971 Super

Bowl-winning team, and later became an assistant of the great coach's staff.

As Ditka grew as a coach, he had one aspiration. He wanted to be a head coach in the NFL, and he wanted it to be for the Chicago Bears. He wrote his old boss a long letter in which he explained his aspirations, apologized for his past feelings, and told Halas how much he wanted to be a Bear once again.

The two had one meeting, and by the time it was over, Ditka was named as the head coach of the Bears prior to the 1982 season.

So began the most raucous era in Chicago Bears history. Ditka was a roaring volcano of a coach, demanding that his players and assistants do things the right way at all times.

He was an old-school disciplinarian who had learned at the feet of Halas and Landry, and he was bound and determined not to let either man down.

The 1982 Bears had endured losing seasons in their previous two years, and Ditka was determined to turn the team around quickly. He pushed his team hard in training camp and began the process of getting rid of slackers. The Bears were 3-6 in that strike-shortened season, but showed signs of progress the following year when they finished .500.

That 8-8 season only fueled Ditka's fire, and he pushed his team harder than ever in 1984. With Jim McMahon at quarterback and Walter Payton running the football, the Bears had a credible offense. However, it was the defense that was really taking shape.

Defensive coordinator Buddy Ryan had a unit that included Dan Hampton, Steve McMichael, Richard Dent, Mike Singletary, Wilber Marshall, Otis Wilson, and Gary Fencik.

The defense was so fast and so aggressive that it was quite brutal to attempt to play against them. Perhaps the best example of this came in Week 9 of that season, when the Bears hosted Archie Manning and the Minnesota Vikings.

Manning had reached the late stages of his career, and his escapability was not what it had been during the prime of his career. The Bears went after him all day, and sacked him eleven times. It was a brutal beating that hastened the end of Manning's career.

It also spearheaded the Bears to a 10-6 record that earned them a spot in the playoffs.

Despite their defensive talent, nobody thought they would be able to give Joe Gibbs's favored Washington Redskins much of a battle in the first round of the postseason. However, the Bears came out of RFK Stadium in Washington with a 23-19 upset. The defense stopped the Redskins and quarterback Joe Theismann when it mattered most, and the Bears earned a trip to San Francisco to face Bill Walsh and his high-powered San Francisco 49ers.

This may have been the best of Walsh's teams, and they laid a 23-0 beating on Chicago. The 49ers would go on to win their second Super Bowl title as they overwhelmed the Miami Dolphins in Super Bowl XIX.

But Ditka would never forget the insult that he perceived Walsh had laid on him in that NFC Championship. Walsh used 300-plus-pound guard Guy McIntyre as a blocking back to help put the game away in the fourth quarter.

Ditka would never forget this, and he would use it as inspiration the following season. The Bears had gotten a taste of success in 1984, but they wanted the full smorgasbord in 1985.

They would run through the NFL in a season that would never be forgotten and would earn the '85 Bears a place in history.

It was a magnificent season that would see the Bears become recognized as perhaps the greatest one-year champions of all-time.

McMahon, though injury-riddled, made it a habit of making big plays when the Bears needed them most. He came off the bench in Week 3 to rally the Bears from a 17-9 deficit at Minnesota to a 33-24 victory by throwing three second-half touchdown passes.

But most of the time, the Bears did not need to rally to win games. They simply pounded opponents with their Payton-led running attack and a ferocious defense that held twelve opponents to ten points or less.

Defensive coordinator Buddy Ryan ran the Bears' 46 defense, and while he and Ditka had little regard for each other as individuals, they formed a remarkable coaching duo.

Ryan's philosophy was to have the defense attack the quarterback at all costs, and the Bears had given him remarkable athletes to accomplish that feat.

The Bears went 15-1 in the regular season, dropping a Monday night game in Miami that remains the highest-rated game in the history of that series.

The Bears had dreams of matching the 1972 Dolphins by going undefeated, but the disappointment of losing in the Orange Bowl did not result in any hangover. They shook the loss off, recorded a video called the Super Bowl Shuffle the next day, and continued their stampede through the league.

Ditka remembered the Walsh move of putting the huge McIntyre in the backfield. He went Walsh one better by putting 325-pound William "The Refrigerator" Perry in the backfield and letting him carry the ball.

"The Fridge" became a cartoon-like symbol for the team, and he was also a fine run-stuffer in the middle of the defensive line.

The Bears shut out the New York Giants and Los Angeles Rams in their two playoff games, and then savaged the New England Patriots 46-10 in Super Bowl XX in New Orleans.

As the Bears were piling up score after score, Payton never got his chance to get into the end zone. That troubled the Hall of Fame running back and Ditka for many years.

"It's something that I wish I could change," Ditka said. "If I knew how much it meant to Walter, I would have given him the ball. But you can't change the past, and you can't live in it."

The powerful Bears would continue to have regular season success as they went 14-2, 11-4, and 12-4 the following three seasons, but they could not get through the playoffs.

Ditka's teams had remarkable talent, but they could not repeat their dramatic regular-season success.

That's part of the reason that Ditka sits at 44th on this list of the best coaches. He had perhaps the greatest team of all time, but he could only coach them to one championship.

The rest of his tenure was disappointing, because championships were the team's only goal and they fell short every year that followed.

But for one year, Ditka was the right coach at the right time to lead one of the greatest teams ever.

For the record

Mike Ditka
Hall of Fame, 1988
Regular-season record: 121-95-0, .560
Postseason record: 12-6, .667
One Super Bowl victory

#45

PETE CARROLL

A Super Bowl win following the 2013 season and a loss in that game the following year have allowed Pete Carroll to raise his professional reputation dramatically.

Prior to the 2013 season, the Seattle Seahawks were moving in the right direction and coming off an 11-5 season that saw them win a wild-card playoff game over the Washington Redskins and fall just short in the divisional playoff game against the Atlanta Falcons.

However, that performance did little to change Carroll's reputation as an excellent college football coach who just did not have all the capabilities needed to win championships at the NFL level.

Carroll heard the doubters, and he knew they existed from the time he was named as the head coach of the New York Jets in 1994. At that time, the Jets responded to Carroll's infectious personality and enthusiasm by winning six of their first eleven games and looking like a possible playoff participant. Instead, the team took a painful defeat at the hands of Dan Marino's Miami Dolphins when the legendary quarterback executed his famed "fake spike" play and threw a game-winning touchdown pass.

The Jets didn't win another game, and Carroll was fired and replaced by (gulp) Rich Kotite, who led the Jets to two of the worst seasons in team history.

Carroll rebounded from the firing and was hired by the San Francisco 49ers as their defensive coordinator. He was successful and parlayed that position to get an offer from Robert Kraft and the New England Patriots. Kraft had just parted company with Bill Parcells, and the owner wanted a coach who was easier to communicate with and less demanding than Parcells.

Carroll fit the bill, and he was immediately welcomed by the Patriots players, who were relieved to be rid of the demanding Parcells.

The Patriots went to the playoffs in each of Carroll's first two years, but they fell to 8-8 in his third season, and the team was trending in the wrong direction. Those same players who celebrated Carroll's arrival in Foxboro soon took advantage of his relaxed attitude. Instead of getting the most out of his players, Carroll's team made multiple mistakes and the two sides parted company.

Carroll took a season off before he was hired at USC, and coaching college football appeared to be the perfect environment for his personality and talent. For one thing, the college game offered Carroll plenty of opportunity to show off his creativity when it came to play-calling and game-planning, and his strong defensive background meant that it would be relatively easy for him to build a team that knew how to stop opponents.

But it also gave him the opportunity to develop his own style. While Carroll never admitted that older, professional players had taken advantage of his relatively easygoing (compared to Parcells and other hard-nosed coaches) nature, he knew he had to alter his ways to prevent that from happening again.

College players were not about to challenge his leadership, and the Trojans were stellar under his leadership, recording an 83-19 record that included a thirty-four-game winning streak and two national championships.

As Carroll grew older and more experienced, he wanted to return to the NFL and conquer a world where he had shown promise but never quite delivered.

The Seahawks came calling prior to the 2010 season, and while it took some time for the Seahawks to turn the corner, they were clearly climbing to elite status.

Carroll's team reached significant heights in 2012, and he knew that his team was capable of winning the NFC West and being able to make a run at the Super Bowl.

Carroll and Seattle general manager John Schneider built the NFL's best defense, and young quarterback Russell Wilson proved to be the perfect triggerman. He was selected in the third round of the 2012 draft, and while few teams saw him as anything more than a backup or a project, Carroll realized that Wilson had all the intangibles— leadership, intelligence, courage—to become a consistent winner.

The only questions were about his physical skills. Wilson was short at 5-11, and there was an impression that quarterbacks under 6-0 could not win. Carroll ignored that, and when he saw that Wilson was accurate, athletic, could throw on the move, and had a strong enough arm, he did not hesitate to make him his starting quarterback.

Wilson was solid as a rookie in 2012, and his play improved significantly in 2013. He completed 63.1 percent of his passes that season and he had a 26-9 touchdown-interception ratio while rushing for 539 yards.

The Seahawks won their division, and they defeated the New Orleans Saints in the divisional playoffs and the San Francisco 49ers in the NFC Championship game.

That game was a huge step, because not only did it get the Seahawks to the Super Bowl, but also it represented a personal triumph for Carroll over San Francisco head coach Jim Harbaugh, his archrival. Harbaugh had been a college coach at Stanford when Carroll was at USC, and they used each other as a measuring stick.

Once the Seahawks survived that battle—a 23-17 win before the team's adoring home fans in Seattle—it was on to the title game.

The Seahawks knew they had been tested severely by the Niners, and they privately doubted that the AFC Champion Denver Broncos would be able to come close to them. They paid the Broncos and quarterback Peyton Manning full respect in the two-week build-up, but they overpowered Denver and rolled to a 43-8 triumph.

Carroll and his players were obsessed with winning a second straight Super Bowl in 2014, but the team was sluggish in the first half of the season. The Seahawks fell to 6-4 after dropping a 24–20 decision at Kansas City.

Carroll got back to basics on offense at that point and turned the offense over to Wilson and power running back Marshawn Lynch, while the defense played back to the form it had in 2013.

The Seahawks won their final six regular-season games, and they dispatched the Falcons 31-17 in the divisional playoffs.

Seattle needed to beat Green Bay in the NFC Championship game at home to get back to the Super Bowl, but all seemed lost late in the fourth quarter when Wilson threw a late interception as the Packers held a 19-7 lead.

Packers players were congratulating themselves at that point, but the Seattle defense stopped Green Bay from earning even one first down, and Wilson scored on a one-yard touchdown run with 2:09 left. The Seahawks recovered the ensuing onside kick and Lynch gave the Seahawks a late lead with a twenty-four-yard touchdown run.

While the Packers would tie the score on a last-second field goal, Seattle won the game in overtime when Wilson hit receiver Jermaine Kearse with a game-winning thirty-five-yard touchdown pass.

The Seahawks were challenged fully in the Super Bowl by Tom Brady, Bill Belichick, and the New England Patriots, but it appeared they would win their second straight title when they had the ball at the New England one with just seconds remaining.

Instead of having Lynch—the game's most ferocious short-yardage back—run the ball in, Carroll had Wilson throw the ball inside to receiver Ricardo Lockette.

It could have been the game-winning touchdown, but New England rookie defensive back Malcolm Butler would have none of it. He undercut Lockette's route and intercepted the pass, giving New England the Super Bowl victory.

Carroll faced criticism regarding the decision head-on and he explained his thought process. He saw the Patriots in what he believed was a goal line defense, so he wanted to take advantage of it by throwing the ball.

Despite this explanation, after the game, the reaction to the play call was immediate and harsh. Many observers described it as the worst play call ever.

Nevertheless, there is no arguing the fact that Carroll has won a Super Bowl, been to another, and won two NCAA championships. As a result, he ranks as one of the NFL's most impressive coaches.

For the record

Pete Carroll
Regular-season record: 83-61-0, .576
Postseason record: 8-5, .615
One Super Bowl victory

#46

BUCK SHAW

Anyone who watches the NFL on even a casual basis knows that professional football is a win-at-all-costs kind of game. Coaches tend to ignore their own players—even their superstars—when they get hurt. When an opponent suffers an injury, there may be some lip service to the media about hoping that player recovers, but there is little sympathy.

It's just the way business is done.

The exceptions to this practice are few and far between. However, Lawrence Timothy "Buck" Shaw was nothing like the standard head coach that stalks the sideline. He was a compassionate man who wanted to win, but he wanted to do it the right way.

Shaw coached the San Francisco 49ers from 1946 through 1954, and held the same position for the Philadelphia Eagles from 1957 through 1960. He was a winning coach with both teams, but his character and decency came out in a late-season game when the powerful 49ers were playing the Cleveland Browns in a key 1948 All–American Football Conference game.

The 49ers and the Browns were the league's two best teams, and the Niners seemed to have the advantage. Not only was the game played at old Kezar Stadium in San Francisco, but also Browns quarterback Otto Graham was playing on an injured knee and was clearly not at his best.

Shaw was not one for speeches to rally his troops—even though he had played college football at Notre Dame under Knute Rockne—but on this day he gave his team instructions on how to play against Graham.

"I want you to rush him hard but fair," Shaw said, in an anecdote reported in *The Eagles Encyclopedia.* "No one is to twist his leg or rough him up. I want us to win this game as much as you do, but there would be no pleasure in victory if we had to cripple Graham in order to win."

The 49ers lost the game 31-28, as Graham threw four touchdown passes. The Browns finished 14-0 that season and won the AAFC's West Division, finishing two games ahead of the 12-2-0 49ers. The Browns completed their undefeated season by beating the Buffalo Bills in the league's championship game.

Shaw's players always had full respect for their coach, even though his priorities seemed to put winning on a lower pedestal than many others. There was an honest, decent, and fair approach to life that very few other leaders in any field—let alone football—came close to matching.

"I played for a lot of coaches in the NFL," said former Eagles receiver Tommy McDonald. "But I can say without a doubt that Buck Shaw was at the top of the ladder. To me, he was the best of them all."

Shaw's 49ers were an excellent team in the four years of the AAFC, but they were beaten regularly by the Browns. San Francisco went 9-5, 8-4-2, 12-2, and 9-3 from 1946 through 1949, and the only year they earned a spot in the postseason was '49.

The Niners beat the Bills in their first-round playoff matchup 31-21, and had a chance to play the Browns in the league's final title game. San Francisco held Graham in check and limited him to 7-of-17 through the air for 128 yards, but Cleveland won the game 21-7.

The Niners struggled to a 3-9 record in their first season in the NFL, but Shaw got them going again in 1951, as they finished with a 7-4-1 record, which was good for second place behind the Los Angeles Rams in the National Division.

The 49ers would continue to win regularly in the NFL for several seasons, but they could never get past the Rams or the Detroit Lions, and did not make it to the championship game. The 49ers appeared to have the best offense on a year-in, year-out basis as they led the league in scoring three times.

They also had a plethora of dominating skill-position players in quarterback Y. A. Tittle, along with running backs Hugh McElhenny, Joe Perry, and John Henry Johnson, but they did not have a balanced team, as their defense often left them short.

San Francisco owner Tony Morabito got tired of watching his team come close but fall short, and he blamed Shaw for the team's inability to win the big games. When the 49ers finished 7-4-1 and slipped to third place in the West Division in 1954, Morabito fired his coach. "It's time we tried something else," were his parting words to Shaw.

Shaw combined college coaching with non-football business interests from 1955 through 1957, but he was lured back to the NFL in 1958 as head coach of the Philadelphia Eagles. Shaw would not take the job until the Eagles acquired veteran quarterback Norm Van Brocklin because he did not want to take the time to teach young quarterback Sonny Jurgensen the nuances of the game.

Shaw almost regretted his decision because the Eagles were awful in '58, going 2-9-1. He was disgusted with his players, many of whom appeared to be mistake-prone, inefficient, lazy, and out of shape, and that was proven by their record. When the Eagles dropped the season finale 20-0 at Washington, Shaw told his players to look around the locker room, because "most of you" will not be back here.

Shaw did as he said in the offseason, and the newly remade Eagles were a hard-working and hustling team that finished 7-5 and earned second place in the East Division.

Prior to 1960, Shaw knew he was tired of coaching in the NFL. He had enough energy to give it one last go-around, but he would not coach in the NFL after that. Van Brocklin came to the same conclusion, announcing that '60 would be his last season as an NFL quarterback.

The Eagles made that year count, as they went 10-2 and won the NFC East by a game and a half over the 10-3-1 Browns. The Eagles had earned a spot in the NFL Championship game against Vince Lombardi and the Green Bay Packers.

Lombardi was in the process of establishing his team as one of the greatest of all time. However, the Packers were a good team at this point in their development and not at their peak. Most observers thought the Packers would come into Franklin Field in Philadelphia and beat the Eagles, but the game was expected to be a close one.

It was close, but it was the Eagles who pulled out the 17-13 decision. Rookie fullback Ted Dean scored the winning touchdown on a seven-yard run with 5:21 remaining, and the Eagles withstood the final Green Bay possession to win the 1960 NFL championship.

The game ended with Philadelphia's powerful linebacker Chuck Bednarik wrapping Green Bay fullback Jim Taylor on the Eagles' nine-yard line as the clock ran out.

"It was the greatest tackle I ever made," Bednarik said.

It also gave Shaw the only championship of his career, as the gentleman coach went out a winner on football's biggest stage.

For the record

Buck Shaw
Regular-season record: 90-55-5, .621
Postseason record: 3-2, .600
One NFL championship

#47

DENNIS GREEN

W hen the career of Dennis Green is up for discussion, one incident comes up more than any other.

As head coach of the Arizona Cardinals in the 2006 season, his team was making a rare appearance on *Monday Night Football* against the 5-0 Chicago Bears. While the Cardinals were just 1-4 at the time, the Cardinals felt they knew the Bears very well because they had played them in the third preseason game that year.

Perhaps even more importantly than knowing the Bears, though, the Cardinals were dominating the game. They built a 20-0 half-time lead, and when placekicker Neil Rackers connected on a twenty-nine-yard field goal with 1:52 left in the third quarter, they had a 23-3 lead.

Under most circumstances, the Cardinals would have been safe to assume that they had secured a victory. Their defense was overwhelming Chicago quarterback Rex Grossman, and the Bears could not move the ball. However, the Bears got two touchdowns from their defense and another on special teams when Devin Hester returned a punt eighty-three yards.

The Bears managed a miraculous comeback and won the game 24-23.

Green was obviously upset that his team blew a chance to knock off an undefeated squad and gain some momentum in the process. He met the media after the game, and as he sat down to answer questions, nothing looked unusual.

But as he began to speak and analyze the game, Green lost control of his emotions. "The Bears are who we thought they were," Green said. "That's why we took the damn field. Now if you want to crown their asses, crown them! But they are who we thought they were. And we let them off the hook."

Green's postgame rant came in the last season of his coaching career, and perhaps all his frustrations came spilling out in that one postgame session. But instead of being a coach who lacked the ability to control his emotions as he was at that moment, he was just the opposite for the majority of his career.

Green had been a college assistant coach at Stanford before he became a head coach at Northwestern in 1981. After a five-year run with the Wildcats, he joined Bill Walsh's 49ers' staff for three years and helped them win a Super Bowl in 1988. From there, he became head coach at Stanford, and took the Cardinals to a bowl game in his third season.

He was viewed as an outstanding coach offensively who also had the skills to become a solid NFL head coach. The Minnesota Vikings came calling in 1992 and made him the second African-American head coach in the modern era.

Green was inheriting a team that had gone 6-10 and 8-8 in the previous two seasons. The Vikings were viewed as a group of selfish malcontents at the time, and Green's goal was to instill an unselfish attitude and promote a team spirit.

Green's enthusiasm set the tone for his new team and the Vikings turned it around immediately. They beat the Packers 23-20 in over-time in the season opener, and they took the momentum from that game to reel off an 11-5 record and win the NFC Central division.

It was a storybook regular season, but the playoffs turned out to be a nightmare. Despite having homefield advantage in their wild-card matchup with the Washington Redskins, the Vikings fell flat and dropped a 24-7 decision.

Losing in the playoffs would become a theme for Green's Vikings. They earned playoff spots in each of the next two seasons, but they went down in the first round to the Giants and Bears in both of those seasons.

Green was undaunted, even after an 8-8 season in 1995 that kept Minnesota out of the postseason. They returned to the playoffs in '96 and lost to the 49ers, but they finally got a playoff victory following the '97 season.

The Vikings were just 9-7 that year and finished fourth in the NFC Central, but that was good enough to earn a spot in the play-offs. Little was expected when they arrived at Giants Stadium to take on the Giants. However, the Vikings roared back from a 19-3 deficit to edge the Giants 23-22 when Eddie Murray connected on a game-winning twenty-four-yard field goal.

While the Vikings lost in the next round to the 49ers, it marked a big accomplishment for Green, as he proved he could finally win a playoff game.

The next season proved to be the Vikings' high point. They already had an accomplished offense with Randall Cunningham at quarterback, speedy running back Robert Smith, and All-Pro wide receiver Cris Carter catching everything he could get his hands on, but the Vikings went to a much higher level when they drafted explosive wide receiver Randy Moss in 1998.

There was no need for Moss to spend time getting acquainted. Green and offensive coordinator Brian Billick quickly recognized that Moss had generational talent, and he caught 69 passes for 1,313 yards and an amazing 17 touchdowns in his rookie season.

Moss was brilliant from start to finish, but he put on his most eye-catching performance on Thanksgiving Day, when he caught three touchdown passes of 51, 56 and 56 yards against the Dallas Cowboys. Moss had turned it up a couple of notches because the Cowboys had bypassed him in the draft and he wanted to show them they had made a mistake.

He clearly made his point.

The Vikings were basically unstoppable that season, as they reeled off a 15-1 record and became the highest-scoring team in league history as they scored 556 points, averaging 34.8 points per game.

They were expected to roll through the playoffs and return to the Super Bowl for the first time since the 1977 season, when they dropped their fourth Super Bowl appearance.

The Arizona Cardinals challenged Minnesota in the divisional playoff game, but the Vikings earned a 41-21 victory.

There were prohibitive favorites over the Atlanta Falcons in the NFC Championship game, and they had a 20-7 lead late in the first half. However, when the Falcons scored in the final minute of the second quarter to make it 20-14, the Vikings appeared to be in shock. They were not expecting a close game.

Late in the fourth quarter, the Vikings sent placekicker Gary Anderson onto the field to turn a 27-20 lead into a two-score advantage. Anderson had not missed a field goal all season, but he hooked a thirty-eight-yard field goal attempt.

The Falcons took advantage by scoring to send the game into overtime, and then completed the upset when Morten Andersen kicked a game-winning field goal and sent the Vikings and their fans home for the season.

Green had two more winning seasons with the Vikings, but it unraveled in the 2001 season. He would take two years off before joining the Cardinals. However, he could not find a winning formula in the desert and he was done at the conclusion of the 2006 season.

The failure of the Vikings to win a championship in 1998 was something Green could not get away from. All the frustration of that defeat came spilling out one Monday night after his team fell apart against the Bears.

It shouldn't obscure the fact that he had a 113-94-0 regular-season record and led his team to the playoffs eight times in the first ten years of his thirteen-year coaching career.

That's an accomplishment that ranks with the top coaches in the game's history.

For the record

> **Dennis Green**
> Regular-season record: 113-94-0, .546
> Postseason record: 4-8, .333
> Four division championships

#48

MIKE TOMLIN

Mike Tomlin was a sharp college assistant coach at Cincinnati in the late 1990s, and his Bearcats went from 111th in the nation in pass defense to 16th. That was all that Tampa Bay head coach Tony Dungy had to see.

He immediately hired Tomlin to coach the secondary in Tampa Bay in 2001, and even though Dungy left the Bucs to take the Indianapolis head coaching position a year later, Tomlin held on to his job.

Jon Gruden was hired as the Bucs' head coach, and he was impressed enough by Tomlin to keep him on his staff. The Bucs went on to win the Super Bowl that season, when their secondary performed expertly.

That got Tomlin noticed around the league, and he was eventually hired as the defensive coordinator by the Minnesota Vikings in 2006. It was just one year later that Bill Cowher retired from the Pittsburgh Steelers, and the confident Tomlin interviewed with the Steelers ownership for the head coaching job.

Many thought he was simply too young—thirty-six—and inexperienced to have a real chance at the position. Many thought that veteran offensive coordinator Ken Whisenhunt had the inside track for the job, but Tomlin blew away the Pittsburgh brain trust—led by owner Dan Rooney—and was named head coach.

Tomlin hit the ground running with his veteran team. One of his key decisions was to retain defensive coordinator Dick LeBeau, who did not have a strategic philosophy similar to Tomlin's. However, the young coach realized that LeBeau had been both highly successful and respected in the Steelers locker room, and he was not about to ignore his attributes in order to show everyone that he was boss.

The Steelers had gone 8-8 in Cowher's last season and many thought the team was on its way toward mediocrity. However, they rebounded to 10-6 in Tomlin's first season, and won the AFC North title.

While they dropped a 31-29 heartbreaker to the Jacksonville Jaguars in the playoffs, Tomlin had given the Steelers a spark.

Quarterback Ben Roethlisberger came of age that season and completed 65.3 percent of his passes, and had a powerful 32-11 touchdown-ratio. Roethlisberger credited Tomlin with much of his development, and the Steelers went into the offseason with a boatload of momentum.

The Steelers went on a roll in 2008, but it was not the result of Roethlisberger's brilliance. He struggled throughout much of the season, and his completion percentage slipped to 59.1 percent.

He also had a hard time hooking up with his receivers on big plays, as he was held to 17 touchdown passes.

But the Steelers made up for the lack of a passing game with a nasty, hard-hitting defense led by James Harrison, who forced seven fumbles that year. The Steelers were a solid 6-3 shortly after the midway point of the season, but they simply caught fire in the second half. They only lost one more game as they rolled to a 12-4 record and another first-place finish.

They picked up hard-earned victories over the San Diego Chargers and Baltimore Ravens in the playoffs to earn a spot in the Super Bowl, and they earned a remarkable 27-23 victory thanks to two spectacular plays.

Late in the first half, the Cardinals were threatening to score and turn a 10-7 deficit into a 14-10 lead. However, Harrison intercepted quarterback Kurt Warner's pass and made an incredible 100-yard return through the Cardinals for a touchdown and a 17-7 halftime lead.

Then, in the final minute of the fourth quarter, Roethlisberger hit Santonio Holmes with a six-yard touchdown pass that proved to be the game-winner.

In just two seasons, Tomlin had taken the Steelers back to the top and he had his Super Bowl. He achieved in two years what Cowher had needed fourteen years to do.

The Steelers missed the playoffs in 2009, but they got back to top form the following year and won the division with a 12-4 record. They beat the arch-rival Ravens in the divisional playoffs 31-24, and then survived a physical duel with the New York Jets to get back to the Super Bowl.

However, the Steelers had a huge assignment in trying to slow down Green Bay's brilliant Aaron Rodgers. While Pittsburgh kept it close and trailed 21-17 early in the third quarter, Rodgers responded with a fourth-quarter touchdown pass and another late drive as Green Bay pulled out a 31-25 triumph.

Few coaches have been to two Super Bowls in their first four years, but that's what Tomlin managed to achieve. His ability to find favorable matchups for his team to exploit was one of his greatest strengths, and he also excelled at firing up his players but not letting them get to the point where they committed foolish penalties that put the team in a hole.

It hasn't been quite so easy in the ensuing four years. While two of Tomlin's teams have made the playoffs, they have not recorded a win since their Super Bowl.

However, there has been a resiliency to both his team and his coaching style. The Steelers have slipped quite a bit on the defensive side of the ball, and LeBeau eventually resigned after the 2014 season.

Tomlin made adjustments to make sure his team was still competitive. The passing game improved, with Roethlisberger throwing to explosive wide receiver Antonio Brown, and the Steelers became a team that showed it could light up the scoreboard nearly every time it took the field.

The Steelers also had a productive running game that could make big plays and take time off the clock.

"In this game you have to make constant adjustments," Tomlin said. "Your players are competing against the best in the world, and we are coaching against the best and most experienced minds in the game. Just because you have had success doesn't mean it will continue. You have to adjust your game plan and then plan your next move. It never stops, and that's the way it always is and always will be."

After the 2014 season came to a conclusion with a wild-card loss to the Ravens, Tomlin said that his passion and feeling for the game was as strong as ever.

"It's still very painful," Tomlin said. "When the journey comes to an end, it should be elation or bitter disappointment, and it is that. We don't run away from that. I embrace that."

He still has many more years to fight for that elation.

For the record

Mike Tomlin
Regular-season record: 82–46–0, .641
Postseason record: 5-4, .556
One Super Bowl victory

#49

TOM FLORES

There were few coaches who had a more difficult assignment going in than Tom Flores when he was named as head coach of the Oakland Raiders.

First, there were the obvious factors. Legendary head coach John Madden had retired after the 1978 season, and all Madden had done in his ten years with the Raiders was become the all-time winningest coach by percentage (.763) in the history of the game. No NFL coach who had been on the sidelines for 100 games or more had ever won with more frequency than John Madden.

The second issue was having Al Davis as his owner. Davis almost certainly knew more about the game than any owner in the history of the league (with the possible exception of George Halas) and he made his feelings known to every coach the Raiders ever had. Many of Davis's thoughts were insightful and invaluable, but what kind of coach can get the job done the right way when his boss is offering his suggestions and input on nearly everything impacting the organization?

But it didn't stop there with Flores. In addition to the pressure of working for one of the most popular and successful teams in the history of the sport, Flores also had to deal with the fact that the Raiders were not the same team when he took over as they had been throughout the majority of the 1970s.

They were getting significantly older, and the difference between the Raiders and their competition in the AFC was growing smaller. The Raiders went 9-7 that year and finished in a tie for third place in the division with the Seattle Seahawks. The San Diego Chargers and Denver Broncos occupied the top two spots in the division, and the Raiders did not even make the playoffs.

Obviously, that did not sit well with Davis, and the 1980 season did not seem like it would be much better. Veteran quarterback Ken Stabler was in New Orleans, and former Houston Oiler Dan Pastorini appeared to have a grip on the quarterback job.

But the Raiders had also brought in thirty-three-year-old Jim Plunkett to compete for a job as a backup quarterback. There were no guarantees Plunkett would even make the team. The former Heisman Trophy winner from Stanford had endured an up-and-down career with the New England Patriots, and while he had a powerful arm, few thought he had the ability to be a winning quarterback in the NFL.

But Flores was happy to have him on board, and when the Raiders got off to a 2-3 start that season, Flores turned to Plunkett to handle the quarterback chores. "He worked with me a lot, to make sure I was confident and comfortable," Plunkett said. "He had been a backup quarterback who had spent a lot of time on the sidelines, so he knew what I had gone through. He helped me and helped our team quite a bit. We were really prepared every time we went on the field."

After Plunkett started to play, the Raiders picked it up considerably throughout the rest of that season. They went 9-2 the rest of the way, and that was good enough to earn them a spot in the postseason as a wild-card team.

They beat the Houston Oilers in the wild-card game by a convincing 27-7 margin, but they appeared to have a rough assignment when they went to Cleveland to take on the Browns. Cleveland was at its best at cold, dank, and cavernous Cleveland Municipal Stadium, but the Raiders were undaunted and pulled off the upset.

They did the same the following week when they upset the explosive Chargers 34-27 in San Diego. Plunkett threw two touchdown passes in that game and also ran for another.

That put the Raiders in the Super Bowl against Dick Vermeil and the Philadelphia Eagles. The Eagles had been the best regular-season team in the NFL that year, and they had beaten the Raiders earlier in the year in a midseason game.

However, the Raiders were a loose, happy, and confident bunch when they went to New Orleans for Super Bowl XV. They knew they had enjoyed a great season and that they were also playing their best football at the time.

While the Raiders were in New Orleans, Flores wanted his players to enjoy themselves as well as prepare for the game. The Raiders practiced hard, but this marauding bunch that included characters like Ted Hendricks, Jeff Barnes, Kenny King, Matt Millen, Lester Hayes, and Todd Christensen also partied hard.

The Eagles did not enjoy the same kind of atmosphere under Vermeil. He wanted his team to be in pristine shape for the Super Bowl, and he ran tight, clock-driven practices and had mandatory curfews for his team.

The Eagles were a finely tuned bunch when they arrived at the Superdome, but the minute they made their first mistake—resulting in a Ron Jaworski interception—the air went out of the balloon.

The Raiders took advantage of every Philadelphia error and pushed the pace throughout the game. The Raiders built a 14-0 first quarter lead on two Plunkett touchdown passes—one of which was an 80-yard catch and run by King—and the Eagles were never able to climb back in the game. The Raiders won 27-10, and in many ways the victory came because Flores had outprepared the meticulous Vermeil.

The Raiders won a second Super Bowl under Flores following the 1983 season. Once again, the Raiders had Plunkett at the helm, and they were a dominating team on both sides of the ball.

After winning the AFC West with a 12-4 record, the Los Angeles Raiders rolled over the Pittsburgh Steelers 38-10 in the divisional playoffs and then beat the Seattle Seahawks 30-14 in the AFC Championship game. That game was particularly satisfying for Flores because the plucky Seahawks had beaten the Raiders twice in the regular season, but could not do it when the money was on the table.

The Super Bowl was expected to belong to Joe Gibbs, Joe The-ismann, John Riggins, and the Washington Redskins, who were trying to defend the title they won the year before. The Redskins went 14-2 in the regular season and had destroyed the Los Angeles Rams 51-7 in the divisional playoffs. They faced a tougher test from the San Francisco 49ers in the NFC title game, but they got by Bill Walsh's team 24-21.

The Super Bowl was expected to be a coronation for the Red-skins, but it turned out to be a 38-9 blowout for the Raiders. The defense smothered Theismann and Riggins, while Plunkett and Marcus Allen were able to punish the once-formidable Washington defense. Allen ran for 191 yards, and his 74-yard touchdown run late in the third quarter remains one of the all-time great Super Bowl plays.

Flores became one of just thirteen coaches who have won two or more Super Bowls. Flores left the Raiders after the 1987 season, but he returned to coaching in 1992 with the Seattle Seahawks. He had three non-descript seasons before retiring for good.

While his years in Seattle were not successful, his legacy was intact. He had proven himself in his tenure with the Raiders—both in Oakland and Los Angeles—and he earned his status as one of the game's top coaches.

For the record

Tom Flores
Regular-season record: 97–87–0, .527
Postseason record: 8–3, .727
Two Super Bowl victories

#50

BLANTON COLLIER

The man should be a legend in Cleveland for what he accomplished while leading the Browns.

As nearly every sports fan knows, Cleveland is one of the hungriest sports cities in the United States. Cleveland fans love their Cavaliers and have a great desire to see the Indians return to glory. However, no team means more to Clevelanders than the Browns, and their fans still have great memories of 1964.

That's the year that the Cleveland Browns won their last NFL championship. They were a smart, athletic, and gifted team, led by the cerebral Blanton Collier.

Collier had been named head coach of the Browns prior to the 1963 season. The team had a relatively young and new owner named Art Modell, who wanted to learn about football from the inside.

Modell thought he had the ultimate insider to learn from in Paul Brown, the team's legendary head coach and the man the franchise had been named after. However, Brown was not interested in sharing his knowledge or his game plan with the team's owner.

Modell was filled with resentment toward his coach. Collier had been Brown's assistant for many years, and Brown respected his knowledge of the game and his ideas. However, when Collier wanted to give Cleveland quarterbacks the option of calling audibles and changing Brown's play calls at the line of scrimmage, the autocratic head coach shot down that idea with fervor.

Modell knew what was going on between Brown and Collier, and he asked the assistant to explain his idea to him. When Collier not only told Modell but showed him on film why the Browns had to give the quarterback the ability to change play calls to defeat the opponent's blitz, the owner was transfixed.

Not only was he learning football from the inside, but also he saw that Brown's old ways were no longer as effective as they had been in the past.

Modell shocked the football world when he fired Brown at the end of the 1962 season and named Collier as his head coach.

Brown had been one of the most innovative head coaches in his prime, and he had a hard time accepting the fact that he could be fired.

But while there was shock in the Brown household and outside of Cleveland, the move was a welcome one inside the Cleveland locker room.

Nobody was happier to see the move made than Jim Brown, the team's outstanding running back. Brown and Collier had an outstanding relationship, and the two thoughtful men had held many discussions about football and all other aspects of life.

Paul Brown had not treated Jim Brown in that kind of manner. The coach treated the superstar running back with little respect as an individual. He treated most of his players in that manner, and that's the way that many coaches treated their players in that era.

However, Jim Brown resented that kind of treatment from his coach, and when Collier was named head coach, the running back felt as if a huge burden had been lifted.

"I loved talking to that man," Brown told Cleveland sportswriter Terry Pluto. "[Collier] had a way of making you feel important. He allowed you to breathe, to grow."

Collier also treated Brown far better than his previous coach had treated him. If the running back needed to rest in practice, he was allowed to do so, without receiving any dirty looks or questions about it.

Collier may not have been the kind of coach who attempted to befriend all his players, but he certainly would make life easier for the players, who were the team's superstars and most important in determining the outcome of games.

Once Collier became the head coach of the team, he helped usher in the modern era of the game. He instituted his audible system, and he had in Frank Ryan one of the brightest quarterbacks the game has ever known running the show.

Ryan was studying for a Ph.D. in mathematics, and numbers were his life before, during, and after his football career. While he played, Ryan appreciated the opportunity to change plays based on the way he saw the defense line up.

Ryan almost always made the right decision when he changed the play call, and that didn't surprise Collier a bit.

The Browns were a strong team in Collier's initial season as head coach, as they finished with a 10-4 record and second in the NFL's East Division. Yet in those days, there was no playoff system. The winner of the East met the winner of the West for the NFL championship, and everyone else went home. That's where the Browns went.

But they were just a tad better the following year, as Cleveland finished with a 10-3-1 mark in 1964 and won the East by a game over the St. Louis Cardinals, who finished 9-3-2.

The Browns earned a spot in the NFL title game against the heavily favored Baltimore Colts, who were coached by Don Shula, the NFL's boy wonder at the time.

The Colts had a team that included Johnny Unitas, Lenny Moore, Raymond Berry, and a ferocious defense led by defensive end Gino Marchetti. The Colts had finished with a 12-2-0 record, and none of the other West Division teams could come close to them. The Green Bay Packers and Minnesota Vikings tied for second with 8-5-1 records.

The Colts came into Cleveland Municipal Stadium with a full head of steam and determined to stop Brown from beating them by running the football. They discounted Ryan and his passing attack. That was a huge mistake.

Ryan threw three touchdown passes that day to wide receiver Gary Collins, and the Colts did not come close to stopping Brown. He carried the ball 27 times for 114 yards, as the Browns were able to move the ball at will.

The Browns also got two field goals from legendary Hall of Famer Lou "The Toe" Groza.

While that was going down, the Cleveland defense did the unthinkable—they blanked Unitas & Co. The final score was 27-0, and Cleveland has been reliving that championship ever since.

There was never any letup from the Browns during the Collier era. They went 11-3-0 the following season, but this time their first postseason opponent was the Green Bay Packers. Vince Lombardi's team had tied the Colts for the West Division title as both teams went 10-3-1, but the Packers emerged from a playoff game to break the tie as they edged the Colts 13-10 in overtime.

The wise guys thought the rested Browns would have a big advantage over their exhausted rivals. In addition to getting the previous week off, the Browns had homefield advantage over the Packers.

It mattered little, as the Packers used the double-barreled rushing attack of Jim Taylor (96 yards) and Paul Hornung (105 yards) to take the Browns down by a 23-12 margin. Jim Brown was held to 50 yards in the final game of his professional career.

Brown's sudden retirement would have caused most coaches to go into shock, but Collier barely batted an eye. He had an exceptional running back in Leroy Kelly, and the Browns continued to win games through the 1960s, even without the greatest back the game has ever known.

The Browns never had a losing season under Collier, and they remained strong contenders. While they lost some of their luster to the up-and-coming Dallas Cowboys, Collier's Browns beat the Cowboys in the newly expanded NFL playoffs in 1968 and '69. However, they were ultimately humbled by the Colts in '68 and the Vikings the following year in the postseason, and those defeats kept them from getting to the Super Bowl.

The Browns slipped to 7-7-0 in 1970, and that was Collier's final year on the sidelines.

He finished his coaching career with a 76-34-2 regular-season record, and his .691 winning percentage is one of the best in history.

Collier was quiet, bespectacled, and to many looked more like a professor than a football coach, but he helped usher in the modern era of football with his stellar coaching.

For the record

Blanton Collier
Regular-season record: 76-34-2, .691
Postseason record: 3-4, .421
One NFL championship

INDEX

Index

Index